This is the second volume of my collection of poems based on my experiences as a soldier in the British Army.

Once again, I dedicate this book to my wonderful wife, Prunella, who like all military wives deserves enormous praise for putting up with the life of a soldier's wife. I also dedicate it to my daughters, Victoria and Jessica and their children and also to my Royal Engineer son-in-law, Warren Whiteman.

I am also grateful to my brother-in-law, David Saunders, for his proof reading of this book.

Military Verse

Volume 2

Clive Sanders

Introduction

I joined the Regular British Army in 1965 at the age of eighteen years and finally retired from the Territorial Army in 2012 at the age of sixty-five years. I am still very proud of my years as a soldier and all the poems in this volume are based on my experiences during those years. I have been very lucky in life and met some of the most wonderful and interesting people through my military career and it is in their honour that I continue to write poems. Hopefully my poems will help them remember some of the memorable experiences that we all lived through during those wonderful years.

Without the brave, interesting and amusing comrades-in-arms I knew during my Army career, I wouldn't have been able to write my poems.

<u>Index</u>

Poems   Pages 1-209

Contents   Pages 211-216

Alphabetical List of Contents   Pages 218-223

I Have Known

I have known gladness and sorrow,
I have known sadness and fear,
If I could start it all over tomorrow,
I would still choose an Army Career.

I have known the deep love of a mother,
I've known the excitement of youth.
I have shared secrets with my brother,
And discovered it's best to tell truth.

I have known the thrills of adventure,
I have known lots of Military pride.
I've done things some people may censure,
But don't care if they're not on my side.

I have known the despair of disaster,
I have suffered unbearable pain.
I have run 'til I can't go no faster,
But I'll try when I run it again.

I have known the glow of succeeding,
I have known the grief of close loss.
I've known broken hearts that are bleeding,
I've felt guilty for showing I'm cross.

I have known the pride of a father,
I cherish the love of my wife,
And I've heard a lot of palaver,
About the true meaning of life.

I have known the sparkle of laughter,
I have known the pleasures of love.
I believe there's a life ever after,
That I'll share with my friends up above.

Band of Brothers

They all joined up together,
At the Recruiting place in town.
They all wanted to be soldiers,
To fight for country, kith and crown.
They completed all their training,
With a smile or with a frown,
And they passed their final exercise,
Spent on freezing Bodmin Down.

They formed a band of brothers,
With agreement from each man.
They'd look after one another,
And protect when others can.
They swore none could be excluded,
They would never face a ban,
And they'd fight for one another,
Like a fearless Scottish clan.

John nodded in agreement,
Charlie gave a little wink,
Ken 'thumbed up' his approval,
Alan asked some time to think.
Reg shouted out "I like it."
Phil wrote it down in ink,
Tom still had his blank look on,
And Sam had another drink.

Those friends split-up years later,
And they went their separate ways,
But they'd meet at their reunions,
And discuss those golden days.
Then Charlie was the last alive,
Good life style always pays,
But eventually his life was gone,
From a string of strange malaise.

John nodded as a welcome,
Charlie answered with a wink,
Ken 'thumbed up' his arrival,
Alan asked some time to think.
Reg shouted out "You're welcome."
Phil wrote it down in ink,
Tom still had his blank look on,
And Sam had another drink.

Stand Up and Be Counted

"Stand up and be counted." Said the Sergeant,
As we lay on our warm Army beds.
The Sergeant walked past every soldier,
And counted as he tapped on our heads.
Then he turned at the end of our billet,
And shouted in his Drill Sergeant's voice,
"We're off on a long winter Route March.
And of that you have no bleeding choice."

"Stand up and be counted." Said the Sergeant,
"The enemy is just one click away.
He plans to kill us with his mortars,
Then charge those who stand in his way.
But you are the men who will beat him.
I've trained you for all of those years.
So just knuckle down to the mortars,
And don't give no ground to your fears."

"Stand up and be counted." Said the Sergeant,
And the men stood who'd lived through the fight.
They looked at the other survivors,
And took stock of the few left in sight.
The Sergeant counted all who were standing,
In his voice that could batter men's ears,
But his men saw how much he was suffering,
Though his voice tried to drown out his tears.

<u>Sharing the Life of a Soldier</u>

It doesn't get talked through when kissing,
It never is mentioned at nights.
That her soldier husband will be missing,
When he flies into combat and fights.

The children are careful when talking,
About Dad when he's faraway.
Mum will give them some news while they're walking,
Home at the end of the day.

Her parents become over-protective.
They buy her expensive new shoes.
Television viewing is selective,
In case something's said in the news.

The calendar has lots of small crosses,
As she counts off the days 'til he's home.
She dreads that she'll hear of some losses,
While she's left in the house on her own.

And then it is finally over,
The kids are dressed up to the nines.
The ferry has docked early in Dover,
So they all hurry down to the lines.

"There is your Daddy." She screams loudly,
The children rush forward to Dad.
He carries them back very proudly,
And for moments forgets what was bad.

The Colonel was telling the Story

The Colonel was telling the story,
Of the Regiment's war in Korea.
He had met quite a few of the veterans,
And made notes with a very keen ear.

"The Regiment was defending a mountain,
Very close to the end of the line.
When the communist hordes attacked with just swords,
Which we thought was an encouraging sign.

They heard the call of a trumpet,
Then the mountain seemed covered in ants.
The Regiment formed an all-round defence,
And ignored all the enemy chants.

Wave after wave bore down on them.
They fired volleys and grenades by the score.
But no matter how many the enemy lost,
There still seemed to be thousands more.

Slowly the Regiment began to lose ground,
And dug-in on the top of the hill.
The Chinese pressed on with their vicious attack,
For no doubt they scented the kill.

The Regiment was surrounded by thousands,
And they fought like the mastiffs of hell.
Then finally died to the very last man.
But they all died so terribly well."

The Mojave Desert

When you first visit the Mojave Desert,
Where the cattle of Arizona graze.
You see the hard rocks of the mountains,
As they silently emerge from the haze.
The desert looks never changing,
And will always look just as it stays,
But the sand changes colour and texture,
The longer you take for your gaze.

For the sun in the Mojave Desert,
Shines a hundred million rays,
That each grain of sand in the desert,
Reflects in a hundred million ways.
And the colour of every reflection,
Changes a hundred million phase,
And the light in the desert has changed like this,
For a countless million days.

The Saint and the Sinner

The Saint and the Sinner had both been one night,
Invited to a grand sumptuous dinner.
This was the first time they ever had met,
For the Saint had a seat by the Sinner.

They started to chat and the Saint started off,
Describing the church he attended.
The Sinner then told of his long army life,
And the chat kind of suddenly ended.

The Saint after a while, told of all he had done,
To campaign for an end to all wars.
The Sinner replied that he had served on campaigns,
To defend those who had a just cause.

The Saint then described how he'd often prayed,
That no tyrant would prosper in life.
The Sinner replied that he'd fought many times,
To protect those affected by strife.

Then the Saint noted the Sinner's hard eyes,
And said, "I pray up to heaven as well."
The Sinner replied, "That it is no surprise,
That I fight to save people from hell."

The Saint thought for a while, then started to smile,
Though he noted the Sinner lacked graces.
The Saint then said, "Forgive me my friend,
For I think that we ought to swap places."

Every Soldier

He was born in every country,
Grew up in every home,
Knew the love of wonderful parents,
Has his stories in many a tome.

He trained with every soldier,
Then travelled to every land,
Was commanded by every General,
Fought every campaign they planned.

He suffered in every battle,
And died in every war,
He tried to live as a hero,
But occasionally broke every law.

He is buried in every country,
And now is remembered by few,
Except for the people he fought for,
And all the old soldiers he knew.

So remember every soldier,
Care for the families they leave,
Help us to honour the fallen,
And pray for the widows who grieve.

His Favourite Armchair

He sat in his favourite armchair,
In the home on the edge of the town.
His pajamas were made of thick cotton,
His slippers were fluffy and brown.
But his mind was out there in the desert,
With his comrades in 3rd Armoured Corps.
They were chatting as they busily loaded,
The shells they would fire in the war.

She brought him a drink of hot chocolate,
And a slice of a nice creamy cake.
She pitied him sat in his armchair,
As she watched, his hand started to shake.
But he was with Alfie and Brian,
As they fuelled up their large Sherman tank.
Alfie was their tank commander,
For he held a Staff Sergeant's rank.

Old Madge was once more complaining,
That she hadn't a spoon for her soup.
She was shouting abuse at her carer,
Whose resistance was starting to droop.
But he was just starting his tank up,
With the sun baking down on his head.
The first tank was leading the squadron,
To the battle that filled him with dread.

She noticed the old man was quiet,
His head lifted high in the air.
His face was gradually whitening,
But his eyes held a cold constant stare.
For the battle had already started,
Shells burst with a frightening crack.
As the nurse fought to restart his heartbeat,
And his eyes closed to hide the attack.

The Sergeant Recruiter

The Sergeant Recruiter looked very impressed,
And said, "I clearly can see,
From the military clothes in which you are dressed,
A soldier you're going to be."

The youth's shoulders went back and he thrust out his chest,
And said, "Sergeant, you can see from a glance,
Since I was a child, there was never a doubt,
I'd be a soldier at the very first chance.

When I finish my training at Infantry School,
I want to be posted abroad.
I'll get a sun tan and sit looking so cool.
I have even bought my own sword."

The Sergeant replied to all he'd been told,
"As a soldier, I think you'll be fine.
But I can't sign you up, 'til your eighteen years old,
But pop back for a chat when you're nine.

The Soldier Enigma

Jock is a soldier and a very hard man,
He can take care of trouble, if anyone can.
But never stand near him, when his knuckles go white,
For it shows that he's angry and getting ready to fight.
Then make sure that you've got a good exit plan,
For blood will be spilt, if you're not in his clan.
You will pray that you make it home safely that night,
As his enemies drop to his skull-crushing might.

But when Jock sees a child that's beginning to cry,
Or is showing distress, there's a tear in his eye.
He's suddenly gentle, and caring, and warm,
But will fight like a tiger, to guard it from the storm.
If a movie is showing about a bird that can't fly,
He'll sob out his heart, trying to figure out why.
And if ever a lady, is threatened by harm,
He will fight to protect her, and be full of old charm.

So be thankful that Jock fought in Afghanistan,
To protect little girls from the dread Taliban.
He fought like a devil, to give them the right,
To be treated as equals in everyone's sight.
And if you have a friend, like Jock there's no ban,
On the good he can do, as a military man.
If you ever think suddenly, you're in a real plight,
It is wonderfully good, to have Jock on your right.

There's a Problem with the Electrics

My wife stood in the doorway,
As I was watching TV,
"That socket in the hallway,
Keeps playing up on me.
Every time I plug the vacuum in,
There are sparks that are clear to see."

I nodded as an advert came on,
And responded to her plea,
"I'll fix it in the morning love,
As soon as I've had some tea."
My wife gave me that peculiar look,
Which puts the fear in me,
And said, I'd rather you paid a man,
To fix it properly."

Ignoring the dig at my manhood,
I responded confidently,
"But it's a simple job my love,
That I can do for free."
My wife thought for a minute,
Then said resignedly,
"Okay, but if you kill yourself,
Don't come running to me."

The Guard on the Gates into Heaven

There's a guard on the gates into Heaven,
To protect it from those who were bad.
So don't mention that your were a soldier,
Or boast of adventures you've had.

Try to stress that you fought for the good guys,
And strived to take care of the weak.
Then smile very hard and mumble some things,
Like you've always behaved very meek.

But surely the guard into heaven,
That's armed with his arrow-filled mags,
Will have been a soldier in his previous life,
So try slipping him a handful of fags.

There Ain't No Use In

"There ain't no use in lying."
Said the Sergeant to Private Lee,
"I can see you haven't shaved today,
You can't hide that from me.
Shave off the bum fluff, you look a scruff.
You horrible little man.
I will make a soldier of you, if anybody can."

"There ain't no use in crying."
Said the Corporal to the recruit,
"Just breathe gently and concentrate,
Every time you shoot.
You've got a good hold; now do as you're told
And squeeze away the shot.
With just a little bit practice, you'll beat this useless lot."

"There ain't no use in dying."
Said the soldier to his pal.
"The helicopter's coming
And you've got to think of Sal.
You've stepped on a mine, but you're doing fine,
They'll fly you home today.
Then he hugged his pal, and he prayed for Sal,
As the pulse slowly faded away.

When I Die

When I die and report to the Guardroom above,
The Orderly Sergeant will say, "We've enough,
Of old soldiers who've passed through these Pearly Gates,
Looking forward to drinking with all their old mates,
But I'm letting you in, so that maybe you might,
Stop all of the others from having a fight.
And if I could ask you, do you think that you would,
Stop them nicking haloes, which belong to the good.
Then perhaps you could get them to stop singing songs,
That offend all the angels in the heavenly throngs.
And one final thing, before I let you in,
Please stop them fermenting that Ambrosia Gin.

Then I'll agree to be good, but when I get inside,
I'll rush over to stand by my mates with much pride.
Then I'll nick lots of haloes and join in the fights,
And I'll sing all those rude songs to fill in the nights.
Then I'll help to ferment that Ambrosia Gin,
That because it's so heavenly, really isn't a sin.
I'll drink lots of spirits, because in heaven they're there,
And laugh as I win in some heavenly dare.
And when God wants a guard, we'll be so neatly dressed,
In immaculate uniforms, that never need pressed.
And so for eternity, in the barracks above,
I'll be surrounded by friends, doing things that I love.

You can always spot a Soldier

You can always spot a soldier,
Even when he's not in kit,
By the way he walks, and the way he talks,
And the way he looks quite fit.

Even when he's left the army,
You can quickly tell the man,
Who has served his Queen and country,
In every way he can.

He will stand whenever the anthem's played,
His chest puffed out with pride,
He normally mixes with his old mates,
Who he has fought beside.

He will easily cry at movies,
That show kids in distress.
He will make enormous efforts,
To clear away a mess.

But there is one thing about him,
Which is loved by all he meets,
It's the stories he can tell his friends,
Of all his glorious feats.

But when he sits with soldier friends,
And they recall a sortie,
The thing that sticks out most of all,
Is that they were sometimes naughty.

For there's a scoundrel in his chuckle,
And a twinkle in his eye,
And a certain pride in the way he looks,
As he goes marching by.

Wesley

Wesley wasn't the best looking soldier,
Or was richly endowed with good looks.
He wasn't the best read young trooper,
Preferred comics to picture-less books.
His youth wasn't spent with nice children,
But with villains and desperate young crooks.
But now that young Wesley's a soldier,
He drives tanks and Land Rovers and trucks.

Wesley wasn't the perfect young soldier,
But learnt as he served through the years.
He wasn't the bravest young warrior,
For he harboured worries and fears.
He wasn't the hardest of fighters,
And would sometimes breakdown into tears,
But now that young Wesley's a soldier,
He really stands out from his peers.

Wesley now is a proud serving soldier,
Who can face any challenge or foe.
He can march many miles in a morning,
Then go where the bravest must go.
He feels pride in the men he calls comrades,
They have courage that few ever know.
So stand clear of each young serving soldier,
He may have some room yet to grow.

When I was a Soldier

When I was a soldier,
I tried to act as tough,
As all the other men I knew,
Who lived and played so rough.
We trained to fight in combat,
And learned the rules of war.
We pushed our bodies onwards,
'Til we could do no more.

Then later I got married,
To my wonderful, lovely wife,
Who joined me on my travels
And shared my Army life.
And now, a lifetime later,
When I think back of those years,
It was she who was the tough one,
Who wiped away my tears.

It was she who stood beside me,
Through times of bad and good,
Who put up with a lot of things,
That no woman should.
It was she who worried if I was safe,
In our quarter on her own.
It was she who brought our children up,
When I was far from home.

She kept our home together,
When my mind was far away,
Thinking of the things I'd seen,
On some half-forgotten day.
It was she who nursed me back to health,
In body and in mind,
It was she who brought me back to earth,
With gestures warm and kind.

So I am very grateful,
For all the things she's done,
I swear that I will make amends,
And try to be more fun.
Now I truly understand,
That all those Army brides,
Sacrifice so much to share
Our travels and our rides.

And when I watch the nation's troops
On each Remembrance Day,
I am proud that I have served my land
And I walked a warrior's way,
But most of all I bless the wives,
Who rarely take the stand,
And weep when the nation honours,
The widows hand in hand.

Sgt. Magonacal Crutch

Soldiers have trust in their Sergeants,
Who teach them the lie of the land.
They respect and obey all their Sergeants,
And follow them closely as planned.
But Sergeant's are occasionally human,
And show they are worth their respect,
But sometimes you do meet a Sergeant,
That truly deserves your neglect.
I once knew a forgettable Sergeant,
Whose legend was not up to much,
The name of this regrettable Sergeant,
Was Sergeant Magonacal Crutch.

This pure unremarkable Sergeant,
Could always get lost with a map,
We hoped when it came to decisions,
Magonacal would be taking a nap.
The officers tried hard to ignore him,
And find some intelligent chap,
For when push came to shove in a battle,
Magonacal would be in a flap.
While others could handle a crisis,
This one man had Jonah's bad touch,
The albatross hanging around our necks,
Was Sergeant Magonacal Crutch.

There has to be somebody somewhere,
Who has just a figurehead role,
For a Sergeant who always is useless
And deserves to be out on the dole.
A Sergeant whose orders are barking,
And conveyed in his best double Dutch,
For the name of incompetence martial,
Is Sergeant Magonacal Crutch.

Lest we Forget

The bugle called softly as the standards dipped down,
In the honour of the war dead from this Somerset town.
Then a silence descended on those stood by the side,
With heads bowed in memory, of those who had died.

As the minutes passed by, they all thought of those men,
Who died for their country, since heaven knows when.
In battles fought bravely, in countries worldwide,
Those men from the county, who had died side-by-side.

But those with their medals proudly pinned on the chest,
Were sometimes seen smiling, to the surprise of the rest.
For in thinking of friends, whose deaths made them sad,
They thought of the good times that together they'd had.

Of friendships they'd made, while they struggled to hide,
Their fears and their worries that attacked from inside.
For even in conflict, when they thought they may die,
There were moments of humour to pass the day by.

So you'll have to forgive if some men on the day,
Are seen to be smiling or looking away.
So let us remember, when we show that we cared,
Lest we forget all the good times we've shared.

I Love my 3-inch Mortar

I love my 3-inch mortar,
And the mortar bombs it shoots,
That land among the enemy,
And kill the nasty brutes.

My lovely 3-inch mortar,
Fires a Shrapnel shell.
It also fires explosive rounds,
And pretty flares as well.

My darling 3-inch mortar,
Is painted NATO green.
And I have stuck some stickers on,
To show where we have been.

I love my 3-inch mortar,
And know that it loves me.
For when I take its cover off,
Its sights light up with glee.

If I were a practising doctor,
I'd be a trained physician.
So when I fire my mortar,
Am I a trained mortician?

The Big Issue

"The Big Issue!" The magazine seller called,
As I approached him that night.
His clothes were quite scruffy; his head was quite bald,
His shirt was a dark shade of white.
But he tried to look proud; he tried to look tall,
If you didn't buy 'The Issue'; that's fine.
But the one thing I noticed about the man,
Was his boots had a hell of a shine.

"Ex-Army?" I asked, as I paid him the coin.
"Royal Signals." He said with a pride.
"Same here." Said I, "What year did you join?"
"Ninety-two. And how my mum cried."
"How long did you serve?" I asked the man.
"Twelve years." He said, with a shrug.
Then he turned away, dropped my coin in a can,
And I walked home feeling strangely less smug.

For the next few weeks I saw him there.
'The Issue' I'd occasionally buy.
Or I'd nod and pass a comment or share
A joke with this ex-Signals guy.
But guilty I felt, with my life so neat,
In my home, with my family about.
While he had no home, he slept on the street,
And for possessions, he seemed to have nowt.

So one night I asked if he fancied a meal,
With my family, at home in our house.
He declined by saying, "Thank you Clive,
But I've a table booked with old Scouse.
I don't like the feel of a family home.
I'm much more at home in my tent.
I only need a few quid, or a very small loan,
For booze, 'cause I don't pay no rent."

Then two weeks later I saw a new man,
Selling Big Issues where my new friend had stood.
And I noticed the 'Liverpool' sign on his can
As he shouted as loud as he could.
So I bought yet another Big Issue,
And asked "Can you please tell me Scouse,
Has your mate moved on or is you,
Meeting him later is some public house."

"Bad news mate, if you're asking after Dan.
He had a turn early morning today.
So I took him to hospital and they tell me they plan,
To operate straightaway.
I'm afraid the booze and the cigarettes,
Will see the end of that man.
He's riddled with cancer and it seems that all bets
Are off, unless save him they can."

In shock I asked Scouse, to which hospital,
They had rushed his old mate.
"He's suffering." Scouse said of his pal,
"I think they are going to sedate."
So next morning I found Dan lying,
In a bed, so clean and so white.
I could clearly see he was dying,
As his face bore the signs of his plight.

But he smiled as he saw me standing,
Beside him at his bed.
And he showed his understanding,
As to me he slowly said.
"I loved Army life." Then he started to cough,
And asked me to pass him a tissue.
"I think my mates are waiting above,
So death is not a Big Issue."

I Love Compo Stew

On exercise in Germany in seventy-two,
We had a nice meal that was easy to do.
You took a big urn and into it threw,
All the things in the Compo box given to you.

Then heat on a burner, 'til it thickens to goo,
And perhaps add a turnip, or mouse, or a shrew.
Then at last when it feels like you're stirring thick glue,
You've finally done it; you've made Compo Stew.

It is good when you're suffering for cold or the flu,
And perfectly complements Wild Boar or Gnu.
Or a roasted Red Deer, or a ram, or a ewe.
But don't add any meat that has patches of blue.

If eaten while hot, it will warm you right through,
And bolster your spirits, so you fight like a Sioux.
Occasionally tough, so may require lots of chew.
Oh I really loved, piping hot Compo Stew.

Alternate Recipe:

If you wanted a change, that was also no worry,
Just add Madras Powder and stir in the slurry.
Then leave it to simmer, for it is best not to hurry,
Then fourteen hours later, you've got Compo Curry.

The Aircraft will Shortly be Landing

The aircraft will shortly be landing,
And then I'll be home from the war.
The families are on the hard-standing,
Waiting to greet us once more.

I know that my wife will be crying,
As she has done on oft times before.
Our national flag will be flying,
To show that we have finished our tour.

The Boeing's tailgate will be lowered,
As the soldiers try to ignore,
The Air Force crew freshly showered,
Who move back as the engines roar.

The families will move forward together,
Looking for the one they adore.
They will bravely ignore the cold weather,
Wearing clothes they just bought from the store.

They will see me supported on shoulders,
As they tenderly bring me ashore.
I will be carried along by the soldiers,
To a military anthem or score.

I will know that my family are near me,
When they carry me out through the door.
My comrades will then carefully place me,
On the hearse's black polished floor.

When You're Young

When you're young and inexperienced,
How do you know what you have missed?
Like the virgin, totally innocent;
Like the frog that's not been kissed.
You must learn from those around you,
Add their examples to your list.
Or try, experiment and flounder,
Surrender, negotiate, resist.

Age will eventually provide you,
With wisdom from both toil and fun.
Lessons from hard work that you've wasted,
Lessons from the things that you've done.
Adventures you have loved or hated,
Adventures under moon and sun.
And then this knowledge with transform you,
To the sort of person young ones shun.

That Certain Feeling

You get that certain feeling,
There's something odd today,
The people in the marketplace,
Looked different yesterday.

There is tension all around you,
There is hatred in their eyes.
There are people glaring at you.
It's you that they despise.

Your heart is beating faster,
Your mouth feels very dry.
You grip your weapon tighter,
You spot somewhere to lie.

Fear is surging through your mind.
You must cast it away.
You decide that if the shooting starts,
It's not you who'll die this day.

You sense that all your comrades,
Have their rifles gripped more tight.
You know they'll stand beside you,
If you have to fight.

You get that certain feeling.
You feel that certain pride.
When you can count one hundred percent,
On those you stand beside.

The Artist and the Tree

The artist sat on Windwhistle Hill,
And quietly took in the scene.
The view was especially colourful,
The air was refreshingly clean.
He was painting the beautiful landscape,
That included both hills and the sea.
And at that particular moment,
He was adding some leaves to a tree.

Painting trees was the thing that in painting,
The artist enjoyed doing most,
As he sat on the top of Windwhistle Hill,
With its beautiful view of the coast.
Just then a feeling struck him,
As he added another leaf more.
He suddenly had the strange feeling,
He had painted this branch once before.

So carefully checking the painting,
He looked for a similar tree,
And eventually found what he looked for,
A twin he believed he could see.
From the easel he picked up his painting,
And carried it down from the hill.
Until he stood by the other tree,
And inspecting it realised the thrill.

No matter what detail he looked at,
He found exactly the same,
On the tree by which he was standing,
As its twin in the picture frame.
Intrigued he searched for something,
That was unique to just one tree.
Then he ran across to the other,
And exactly the same detail he'd see.

And so for the rest of the morning,
He walked from one tree to the other.
Every aspect he looked at on one tree,
He found just the same on its brother.
The one thing he found most amazing,
Was a Love-heart carved in one tree.
And when he checked on the other,
There was 'FM loves KP'.

Now tired from all the walking,
He sat on a convenient mound,
And slowly thought of all the odds,
That ruled out what he had found.
And then he thought of a trial,
As he stared at the tree on the crest.
He had a saw in the boot of his car,
Which would put the trees to the test.

And so he marched back to his car,
And the saw from the car boot he drew.
He would cut-off a branch from one tree,
Just to see what the other would do.
So he walked to the tree at the top of the hill,
And cut down a substantial limb.
Then walked across to the other,
To see what had happened to him.

His wife became worried that evening,
When the artist was late home for his tea.
So she drove to the top of Windwhistle Hill,
And found him crushed under a tree.
The police investigated the accident,
And the inquest complied with the law,
The artist had clearly died tragically,
When he'd cut off the branch with his saw.

(Continued on next page)

The artist was buried one week later,
And his widow disposed of his things.
She burned the last landscape of Windwhistle Hill,
Along with the memories it brings.
So no one ever looked at the painting,
So no one ever took the blame,
For not noticing two trees in the picture,
Were painted exactly the same.

I Miss All Those Comrades I Had

It is now many years since my old Army days,
And I miss all those comrades I had.
We tried to behave in the best Army ways,
But occasionally did things that were bad.

We'd drink and we'd fight, then we'd drink even more,
Then we'd prepare for our next round of fights.
Our excuse was that were getting ready for war,
When we'd probably die protecting your rights.

But we're now growing old and we're missing old friends,
That have died in such horrible ways.
And we know that it's merely the way that life ends,
And think back to those good Army days.

As we now tell each other, we are not feeling well,
And the list of old friends is depleted.
They are probably right saying, "We'll all go to Hell."
But we'll soon have the Devil defeated.

The Bloody Afghan Desert

The Afghan desert is stony hard,
And devoid of all comfort and life.
And the future now seems exactly the same,
For the young dead soldier's wife.

There's a crater in the rocky path,
Where her soldier-husband fell.
There's a hole as big as the desert,
In his family as they bid farewell.

There's a ghost in the Afghan desert,
That knows he should be at home.
But he can't rest 'til his duty's done,
So he'll fight on all on his own.

The wind blows over the desert,
And the blood stain fades away.
But the memories his family holds on to,
Grow stronger every day.

There's a ghost in the Afghan desert,
At the spot where the soldier died.
That will never surrender to terror,
But stands-fast with a soldier's pride.

So what is your Idea of Heaven?

So what is your idea of heaven?
How do you hope it will be?
Out of five, will you rate it at seven?
Or will you just wait and then see?

Although I'm in no rush to get there,
I'm confident of what I will find.
There will be a cold beer by my armchair,
With a snack of the savoury kind.

My chair will be fluffy and snugly,
All my friends will be standing close by.
The ladies will be lovely, not ugly,
And the sun will shine high in the sky.

I will have all my family around me,
Or those who have gone on before.
The ones I don't like, I just won't see,
I'll just see the ones I adore.

Each morning I'll rise by ten-thirty,
Then I'll laze, 'til it's time for my lunch.
I'll eat crayfish, but never get dirty,
And enjoy the odd glass of nice punch.

Wings I will not be a-wearing,
My voice will keep me out of the choir.
I'll probably be occasionally swearing,
But it will never drop me in the mire.

For me heaven will be how I want it,
Like a pub, with endless free beer.
It will never be boring, not one bit,
But for now, I will not volunteer.

The Medals on your Chest

The Remembrance Day parade,
Passed through the Somerset Town.
The old man had dressed smartly,
But the rain had hammered down.
When a mother with a young boy,
Said, "My son is most impressed.
He says you are a soldier brave,
'Cause you've medals on you chest."

The old man smiling broadly,
Shook the young boy's hand.
And said, "I was a soldier son,
And led a life so grand.
I have known a lot of soldiers,
With more courage than I possessed,
Who should be here beside me,
With their medals on their chest.

But the medals that I wear proudly,
Are for the time I've done,
And all the places I have been,
Before you were born my son.
Perhaps you'll be a soldier,
And stand out from the rest.
Then when you are as old as me,
You'll have medals on your chest."

The young boy then stepped forward,
And asked if he could touch,
The medals that the old man wore,
With pride that showed so much.
The old man explained the medals,
On the coat in which he was dressed,
And the reason he'd been awarded,
The medals on his chest.

Then the boy looked to his mother,
And in a voice not very loud,
Said, "If Daddy was alive today,
He would be standing proud.
For Daddy was a soldier,
But died in Baghdad West,
Or he'd be here beside me,
With his medals on his chest."

We were never the Bravest of Heroes

We were never the bravest of heroes,
That our nation had ever seen.
Our bank accounts averaged at zeroes,
But our boots were occasionally clean.

The Army had made soldiers of us,
Cruel life had taught us to fear.
We'd the guile of an innocent novice,
Though we drank many gallons of beer.

We pretended that we all had lovers,
For the girls like a uniformed man.
We envied the seniors above us,
But strived hard to defeat every plan.

We sniggered at those who commanded.
We ridiculed Sergeants each day.
We only did what life demanded,
And would dodge work, if we found a way.

But somehow we worked well together.
Sometimes the Army was right.
We would practise in foul or cold weather,
For when we were needed to fight.

And when we deployed in a crisis,
We would fight to our preconceived plan.
The men I stood by weren't the nicest,
But I wouldn't have changed any man.

Mustaffa

John is now five months
Into his final Afghan tour.
He hopes it will the the last time
That he has to go to war.
But John now has Mustaffa,
As his very closest friend.
And keeps Mustaffa close
To stop him going round the bend.

Steve is in John's platoon,
And has the next door tent.
He thinks that John is deviant
And obviously bent.
Steve thinks it clearly isn't right,
And is certainly remiss.
He's not keen to see them fondle
And hates it when they kiss.

Mustaffa knows no English
And John can't speak Afghan,
But somehow they communicate,
In any way they can.
Steve doesn't mind it when
John pats Mustaffa on the head,
But thinks that it's immoral
When Mustaffa shares John's bed.

John dreams about Mustaffa,
And cares for him a lot.
He hopes that when he flies back home,
Mustaffa won't be shot.
He loves Mustaffa dearly
And often they will snog,
For Mustaffa is a special friend
And a lovely little dog.

Last Man Standing

The churchyard was empty, except for a man,
Sitting quietly and deeply in thought.
I watched for a while and then forming my plan,
I asked if I could enter his court.

He looked up and smiled and nodded his head,
And moved to the left on his bench.
I sat down and after a few moments said,
"They've made a good job of that trench."

He nodded and then looked me straight in the face,
And said, "These men, I was proud of commanding.
But now they've all gone to that higher place,
And I'm left as the Last Man Standing."

We first got together in southern Iran,
Where we picked up new tanks in the port.
And then we were shipped to a port in Sudan,
Then all through the desert we fought.

We thought we were lucky, for we suffered no dead,
Although there was always a stench,
That just hangs around, when somebody's bled,
And often made my stomach wrench.

And then back to Blighty, where we would replace,
Troops who died in the Normandy Landing.
And there they were killed by a famed Panzer Ace,
And I was left as the Last Man Standing.

Letter Home – April 1945

My dearest darling Janet,
I'm fine, so don't worry about me.
But yesterday we came on a prison,
That people at home ought to see.

The war can't go on too much longer,
So, with luck, I will shortly be home.
We've the rest of our lives together,
Just the two of us and our baby Jerome.

Last week we fought through to Celle,
And took it on April the twelfth.
Only a few of the buildings are damaged,
And the people are in pretty good health.

But not many miles further eastwards,
We came on this terrible place,
Where people have been treated so badly,
That the whole world will think a disgrace.

The camp's at a place they call Belsen.
It was run by the German SS.
You should see how the people have suffered.
It is just one horrifical mess.

The prisoners were starving and beaten.
There is typhoid all over the camp.
They had to sleep in terrible conditions,
With filth, disease, cold and damp.

People are still dying of starvation.
We've been told not to give them much food.
We are trying to give some medicine,
But all that we've got is so crude.

It's the women and children that upset me,
They are thin as the teeth on a comb.
Every time I look at their suffering,
It reminds me of you and Jerome.

What Do Soldiers Do?

In the pub yesterday,
For just one or two,
When the question was asked,
"What do soldiers do?"
The question's quite simple,
But after some thought,
I replied with my answer,
"Try not to get caught."

The truth of the matter,
Is hard to get to,
For I don't think there's a plan,
For what soldiers do.
They eat and they sleep,
And some skills they are taught,
And they have lots of leave
And they do lots of sport.

Soldiers are sometimes naughty,
Which really isn't so new.
They buy the cheapest whisky,
Or even make up their own brew.
They get a train ticket to Rugby,
But then travel on to Newport.
They romance the willingest ladies,
And then try not to get caught.

They drink lots of beer
And they eat lots of stew,
And they tend to hang out
With the rest of their crew.
They spend all their money,
'Til they're left with nought,
Then they go back to camp
And regret what they've bought.

But occasionally they have
Their real job to do,
To fight for their country;
For me and for you.
And when combat is joined
And battles are fought,
They do what they do
And try not to get caught.

Posted to Afghan

Brian wasn't really pleased
To be posted to Afghan,
But being a professional soldier,
He took it like a man.
He trained for months before his unit
Started on their tour.
He felt the sense of duty
That he always felt in war.

He quickly settled into life
In his forward fighting base.
He liked the sunny weather
That had quickly tanned his face.
He learned to speak a few words
In the local native tongue.
He got on with the Afghans,
Especially the young.

He was worried about the IEDs
And mortars from afar.
He grew to be quite twitchy
When walking past a car.
He lost a friend to sniper fire
When he'd just been there a week.
He ducked down only just in time
As the bullet passed his cheek.

Every week he sent a letter home
To his loving Mum and Dad.
He told them of the things he'd seen.
Some good and some quite bad.
He liked it when they told him
Of the homely things he missed.
His mother sent him home-cooked cakes
That he could not resist.

He sent his parents presents;
They liked the Afghan rugs.
He also sent them T-shirts
And the usual unit mugs.
They were planning a big party,
For when he came back from his tour,
Which made the shock more terrible,
When the knock came on the door.

Military Intelligence

The purpose of Intelligence is to analyse the gen.
And then to brief the General of the where and when.
So he can tell his officers, where to place their men,
And we can have a cup of tea, before he's back again.

They're Home!

The flags fluttered proud,
All the families were there.
The children cheered loud,
There was joy in the air.

The bus slowed down,
Then stopped with a sigh.
To the officers' frown,
Wives started to cry.

"They're home!" was the shout.
"There's Daddy and John."
Proud parents called out,
As they spotted their son.

The doors open wide.
Brave soldiers climb down.
They form ranks side-by-side.
They're the pride of the town.

And Jenny holds tight,
To the arm of her Dad.
"We'll be back home by night,
And I won't be so sad."

But for some there will be no welcoming back.
As their husband or father or dearly loved man,
Was killed by a landmine or a frenzied attack,
On their last tour of duty in Afghanistan.

The Most Expensive Gift

A good boarding school in Surrey
Took the girls out for a ride.
They planned to visit Margate
And would be there before high tide.
The girls were discussing presents
As they listed them with pride.
Naomi said, "What was the nicest gift
That your Daddy ever buyed?"

Priscilla said, "A diamond.
For on the day I am a bride,
I will wear a gold tiara
With the diamond set inside."
Hermione said, "My pony,
For when I sit astride,
I can feel his strength between his legs,
Like a raging bull untied."

Angharad said, "My mobile phone,
Which I rarely lay aside.
That lets me chat with all my friends,
At home or spread worldwide."
Cleo said, "A plot of land,
That stands by the River Clyde.
That when I grow up, will be the place,
Where I will then reside."

Naomi then turned to Sarah,
And in a voice both cruel and snide,
Said, "Sarah, has your family
Ever made your eyes grow wide,
By giving you an expensive gift?
The best you ever spied.
For we know your family are not rich,
Or own much countryside."

Sarah looked at Naomi
And ignored the hurt implied.
Then answered in a steady voice
That was steadfast in its pride.
"My Dad gave me my freedom."
Sarah quietly replied,
"And the price my family paid for that?
My soldier father died."

When I Die Please Do Not Grieve

When I die, please do not grieve,
For I will not be dead.
I'll be on reconnaissance,
To see what lies ahead.
Then when I've found the safest path,
I will wait for you.
To meet you when you're on your way
And safely guide you through.

I'll find you a billet,
Where you can lay your head.
On the softest pillow I can find,
On the most luxurious bed.
The window of your billet
Will have a lovely view,
Of perfect English countryside
And warming skies of blue.

So don't you shed a tear for me,
For death has lost its dread.
I've had a wondrous journey
And I'm pleased with where it led.
Then I'll be waiting patiently,
For when your trip is due,
And lead you along the easy path,
As your faithful guide so true.

When You Are Young

When you are young
And invariably right,
You don't mind the pain
And enjoy a good fight.
You can work through the day
Then dance through the night,
In pursuit of a girl
And the hope that she might.

Then you are married
And become a dad.
And you fight to protect them
From everything bad.
You work to give children
All that you never had,
Or at least, give them things
That will make them feel glad.

Then you are old
And you simply don't care,
That your waistband's expanding
And you've got greying hair.
Your children complain
Of the clothes that you wear,
And you coolly respond
With a withering stare.

And so life's complete
And you've run a good race.
The worries of life
Are marked deep on your face.
You still want to compete,
But you can't stand the pace,
But you'll never give in
Without showing bad grace.

Yesterday, Today and Tomorrow

Yesterday is already behind us,
But the memories are still close to mind.
Some are glorious warm memories of comfort,
That straight to our hearts are consigned.
Some were dreadful moments we've lived through,
That we try hard to leave far behind.
But we must take forward the lessons,
With the good ones we've learned underlined.

Today is still all around us,
The colours are strong to our eyes.
And yesterday's lessons prepare us,
So there shouldn't be any surprise.
Because we've seen both joy and sorrow,
We are now able to strongly advise,
Those who struggle to live for tomorrow,
So success they will win as their prize.

Tomorrow should bring love and excitement,
It's a contract that's yet to be signed.
With the wisdom of yesterday's lessons,
Our future can be more refined.
And we who have lived through great sadness,
Must refuse to be undermined,
But to build on our hardened foundations,
So tomorrow should prove to be kind.

If You Meet A Soldier

If you meet a soldier on your trip to the pub,
You should buy him a pint, not give him a snub.
But if it goes down in a second or two,
Don't buy him another, whatever you do.

Then ask him about all the places he's been,
All the foods he has eaten; all the sights that he's seen.
And here is a tip for the rest of your life,
Don't let him stand next to your good looking wife.

Don't challenge a soldier to some drinking game,
You'll end up unconscious, or dying of shame.
And don't let him get angry, please just treat him right,
Or you'll get involved in a terrible fight.

Ask him quite early, what cap badge he wears,
And try to ignore every time that he swears.
For his swearing he heard in recruit training days,
From some old Sergeant Major, as critical praise.

He tries to be good, but the effort soon hurts,
He attracts lots of girls, in very short skirts.
His tattoos tell stories, of far-away places,
And often show ladies, or crosses, or aces.

But a soldier's a friend, who we all like to know,
Who'll stand by your side and trade blow for blow.
He's a qualified hero and a much cherished son,
But an angel's certificate, he's still working on.

Enjoy your Sweet Dreams

The child was sleeping and dreaming sweet dreams,
About her mother and father and home.
Her father would kiss her and tell of his schemes,
As he went through her hair with a comb.

Her mother would laugh at her father's jokes,
Her sister would hum to his songs.
Her brother would rebel to his father's hoax,
And sulk at what he thought were wrongs.

But her father will never again come back home,
He was killed in an artillery attack.
Her mother was killed when the cathedral dome,
Collapsed with an awful crack.

As a Christian family in the Syrian war,
Her family lives in terror each day.
Her sister stands in line for many hours more,
Begging food, or stealing it away.

Her brother now fights to protect their town,
They haven't heard from him in weeks.
The constant worrying is getting her down,
There are tracks of tears on her cheeks.

So dream on little child of the Syrian war.
But dream not of the fighting and screams.
Dream on of the sister you will always adore,
And for now just enjoy your sweet dreams.

I Have Never Told Others Your Secrets

I have never told others your secrets.
I have kept all your assets secure.
For years I have cared for your treasures,
And would do for many years more.

But you've see another, that's younger.
My looks are no longer in style.
I know that you want to replace me,
I've been feeling unloved for a while.

I've been there by your side while you're sleeping.
I never complain when you snore.
I'm upset for you when you are weeping.
I stand between you and the door.

I love it when you run your hands up me.
I swoon when you give me a smile.
She will never love you just as I do,
And I think that her smell is just vile.

Please do not throw me out of your bedroom.
Please do not throw me out in the cold.
I know that you not longer love me
No one loves a wardrobe that is old.

I Have Lived Amongst Men

I am honoured to say, I have lived amongst men,
Who have stood by my side and would do again.
We trained to be soldiers; we learned to be friends,
We faced life together, all that fate ever sends.
I struggled to be as brave as the rest,
Then I conquered my fears and I passed every test.
I was proud in their company, especially when,
We stood shoulder to shoulder. I have live amongst men.

The men I called comrades during all of those years,
In fun and in laughter, in horror and tears,
Were the best that our country could ever have raised.
We were cursed by opponents, then occasionally praised.
We fought for the causes, we thought were the good.
We held our positions and died where we stood.
I rejoice in my memories, I recall now and then,
For I followed the code and I have lived amongst men.

Job Interview

The manager said, "We're impressed with you Fred.
Tell us about your life story.
Your CV tell us, that you don't like a fuss,
But tell us a bit of your glory.

The ex-soldier said, "I was born in Hampstead,
And grew up in Clacton-on-Sea.
I can't do calculus, but saw an ad on a bus,
And signed up for a life military."

"I have fought in two wars, on operational tours,
And now have a medal or two.
I have commanded real men, and proved time and again,
That I can make most of a crew."

"I don't have a degree, my education was free,
I've not sat in a punt on the Isis.
But I hope you will see, that a soldier like me,
Can be really good in a crisis."

Poet's note:- I hope he got the job!

King Arthur Awakes!

In the hill above Avalon,
Something stirs, something quakes,
King Arthur of Camelot
Feels trouble and wakes.
He senses a threat
To his kingdom of old,
And he long-ago promised
To wake from the cold.
He swore he'd protect
His old kingdom from harm,
As he slept in the hill
Due to old Merlin's charm.

And now there's a threat
From a fanatical horde,
Who want to convert
By the power of the sword.
There's no love and no honour
In the life that they lead,
They distort and corrupt
All who follow their creed.
They murder and slaughter
All who do not agree,
With their fanatical view
Of the world that they see.

But King Arthur now senses
There are many who'll fight,
For the safety of England
And to preserve all that's right.
There's an Army well trained
To defeat evil men,
And a Navy to protect
Our borders from when,
These fanatics attempt
To land on our shores,
With plans to kill all,
Who live by God's laws.

The Air Force will guard
All who fly in our skies,
And Marines will fight
Everyone in whom evil lies.
The police and the public
Will support in the war,
All those who fight evil,
In the name of the law.
But King Arthur's heart bleeds
For those who have died,
Facing evil fanatics,
Who have few on their side.
But he can foresee
A future that's bright,
For his kingdom will eventually
Prevail in the fight.
And thanks to the powers
That old Merlin gave,
He can safely return
To sleep quiet in his grave.

The Sergeant's Men

The Sergeant watched his soldiers,
And he muttered 'neath his breath,
"This useless bunch of idiots,
Will surely be my death.
Their brains are clearly empty,
And they're dreadful on the square,
If Social Workers see them,
They will put them all in care."

Then only two months later,
They were posted to Iraq.
They'd only just got into camp,
When they had their first attack.
They fought a four month battle,
But they never lost a man,
For all the Sergeant's soldiers,
Worked exactly to his plan.

Then home to tea and medals,
And the Colonel tapped his chest.
"You must tell me how you trained these men,
Who clearly are my best."
The Sergeant walked back smiling,
Then he turned and faced his men.
"Whoever nicked the Colonel's hat,
He'll want it back again."

Let the Children Play

As a child I was more than just lucky,
Our house had just behind,
The most adventurous playground,
That a boy could ever find.

It had been made by the German Air Force,
Available by day and by night.
You see my favourite playground,
Was a carefully constructed bombsite.

The treasures that we could find there,
Were priceless beyond all worth.
There were shrapnel, shell splinters and bullets,
Scattered around in the earth.

We children would all play together,
Ignoring all safety rules,
Mostly at weekends and evenings,
When we were let loose from the schools.

But today I fear all our children,
Aren't allowed the adventures we knew.
They are children of Gameboys and Ipads,
With only a digital view.

And there are many countries,
Where children are robbed of their youth.
Fighting for just their survival,
Or learning what they're told is the truth.

So my plea is so glaringly obvious,
Please let all the children play.
And then they can later discover,
The horrors that will come their way.

Listen!

Listen, can you hear them,
The sound of silent screams.
The noise of countless victims,
Who were robbed of all their dreams.
They are screaming in their grave yards,
And from every unmarked grave.
They are screaming for the ones they loved,
That no one tried to save.

Listen to their sufferings,
The roars of silent rage.
From Auschwitz, Srebrenica, Cambodia,
Or other murdering cage.
Things we thought were over,
At the end of Hitler's days,
Are still going on in places new,
And in most barbaric ways.

Then listen to the silence,
Of the prayers and the dreams of youth.
They must learn of the sufferings,
And be told of the dreadful truth.
But then let them go forward,
And pass to them the rope,
So that they can drag us onward,
For they are still rich in hope.

Love is not like a Burger

Love is not like a burger,
Served with pickles and cheese,
That looks so good in the advert,
Then only gives seconds of please.
Love is not like a burger,
Served with mayo and fries,
That is cheap, that is fast, that is over,
And all of the experts despise.

Love is not like a Hot Dog,
Served from a stand on the street.
That smells so good when you're passing,
Then tastes like warm boiled meat.
Love is not like a Hot Dog,
Served on a white paper sheet,
That satisfies only for seconds,
Then leaves you empty replete.

Love is not like a Pretzel,
Twisted and baked hard outside.
Love is more convoluted,
But is worth all the effort inside.
Love is not like a cheesecake,
That tastes so good at first bite.
Love tastes good for very much longer,
Unless it is just for the night.

Love to me is Roast Dinner,
That takes so long to prepare.
But the reward is just everlasting,
It is worth all the hours of care.
Love to me is Roast Dinner,
Cooked on a low simmering heat,
That gently warms every bit of your soul,
From your head to the tips of your feet.

A Brave Shoulder of the Queen

My mother, God bless her, when she was alive,
Would tell others a story, of when I was just five.
If asked what I'd be when I'm older,
I'd look up and I'd stare in the old person's eyes,
And answer the question, with a look of surprise,
"I just want to be a brave shoulder."

The old person would laugh at my simple mistake,
If nice they would buy me a lovely big cake,
And say, "A shoulder is not what you'll be.
I suspect you were thinking of a different word,
That's similar in sound, when originally heard,
But I think a brave soldier we'll see."

I signed up for the army at the age of eighteen,
To fight for my country, my land and my Queen,
And was proud of the man I'd become.
I was trained to survive and to fight in a war,
And prepared for the horrible things to be saw,
That brought terror and horror to some.

Then many years later in a Bosnian town,
With Serbian snipers firing straight down,
Where a road was a place people die on.
I tried to bring comfort to the people I met,
In a town that today people seem to forget,
And became a brave shoulder to cry on.

Autumn's Last Leaf on the Tree

The old man stood alone in the church yard,
By the memorial for the men of the town,
Who had died in those dreadful conflicts,
While fighting for the nation and crown.

He read through the names of the fallen,
Nodding when he could picture the face.
He would smile at some long ago memory,
Of good times in a faraway place.

He noticed me watching him smiling,
And said, "I remember these men.
I served with old Alf in the desert,
Then he died, but I can't recall when.

Me and young Sid were just school boys,
Who joined up when we were sixteen.
We were in the same company at Anzio,
Where he was shot in the stomach and spleen.

And now they've all gone to their maker,
And the last one surviving is me.
I'm the last of that great band of brothers.
I'm autumn's last leaf on the tree.

I look down at my fallen companions,
Who are free from the will of the fates.
And now I look forward to falling,
And finally rejoining my mates."

Did You Sleep Well My Darling?

"Did you sleep well my darling?"
The wife asked her man.
He smiled as he answered,
"As best as I can."

She rose and she made him,
A nice cup of tea.
Then asked him, quite nicely,
"Were you dreaming of me?"

He looked up at his wife,
Then with eyes full of pain,
Replied, "I was dreaming my love,
Of our honeymoon in Spain."

She had noticed his eyes,
The pillow carried a stain.
So she quietly said,
"You were crying again."

"I'm sorry my darling."
The man said to she,
"I just keep remembering,
That patrol in Newry."

His wife held him tight,
As the shaking began.
Then it was she who was crying,
For her old soldier Stan.

Christmas in Bethlehem

In Bethlehem town, two millennia ago,
A saviour was born, or we believe so.
To bring us salvation, from all that is bad,
Do you think that our saviour is now pretty sad?

He's watched over that town and saw the years flow,
And hate fuelled the flames of war that still grow.
The tidings he brought us, to make us all glad,
Were swamped by the suffering, this small town has had.

The Romans, Crusaders and Muslims all know,
They've fought for the town, since times long ago.
So surely our Lord, will now think us all mad,
Unless we can settle, all the issues we've had.

Then perhaps we can have a new saviour so,
We can all pray together, side by side, toe to toe.
And Bethlehem town, with lights will be clad,
While angles in Heaven, glad tidings will add.

Falkland Islands Grass

In the Falkland Islands,
Grass grows everywhere.
You can walk on the tufts,
But must always take care.
For it rips through your boots,
And the clothes that you wear,
And it slashes your skin
And gets stuck in your hair.

It grows very tall,
In the cold windy air,
And its blades are as sharp
As a fresh Prickly Pear.
But to hard Upland Geese,
It's a soft comfy chair,
On which they build nests,
Made of grass and of hair.

There are places in the Falklands,
That are rocky bare.
Where troops fought and died,
In the light of a flare.
They believed in their cause,
But they thought it unfair,
That it was they who were fighting
And paying their share.

Those that survived
Now recall the despair,
And the fear that they felt,
In the searchlight's bright glare.
They hugged the sharp grass
In the battle's loud blare.
They stayed still under fire,
Then advanced when they dare.

Some were buried on the islands,
After a service or mass,
And they lay in their graves
Side by side, class by class.
Now the graves show the signs,
Of the years as they pass,
And the flowers are replaced
By the harsh Falkland's grass.

And the Soldier Cried

The girl hugged her doll as she stared at the floor,
At the corpse of her mother all covered in gore.
Her silent tears of helplessness tore,
At the heart of the soldier who stood at the door,
And the soldier cried, and the soldier cried.

Years passed oh so fast, 'til the soldier's next war.
In a country, so scarred, with a people so poor,
And the suffering returned, but this time much more,
And the sergeant was shocked by the things that he saw,
And the soldier cried, and the soldier cried.

Now retired and alone at ten years and three score,
The soldier's mind dwells on those years long before.
And the memories come back of the horrors of war,
Of the girl with her doll and her mum on the floor,
And the soldier cried, and the soldier died.

Don't!

"Higgins!" The sergeant shouted out,
"It's no good you trying to hide.
You won't find a place that I can't see,
Then I'll kick your fat backside."

"Don't point a rifle at anyone,
Unless you intend to shoot.
For if I ever see you do it,
You'll feel the sharp end of my boot."

The sergeant was not in the best of moods,
That was clearly plain to see.
But as Higgins was his sole target,
He was taking the grief off of me.

"Don't think of showing me any cheek.
Don't ever attempt to dispute,
Any order or task that I give you,
Or I'll squash you like a newt."

"Higgins," the sergeant was losing his grip,
"You horrible excuse for a man.
Your heart from your chest I'm intending to rip,
Then sauté it slow in a pan."

"Keep clear of my house by several miles,
Or you'll feel such a wealth of sheer pain.
And never respond to a young lady's smiles,
Or kiss my young daughter again."

Here I Lie

(For Warren)

Here I lie in my mother's arms,
Warm, content and well fed.
Blissfully unaware of the hardships,
I'll face in my life ahead.

Here I lie in my lover's arms,
As she gently strokes my head.
How can anything be this nice?
Snuggled-up warmly in bed.

Here I lie in my family's arms.
After bringing home their bread.
Let me protect them from all harms,
And suffer in their stead.

Here I lie in nature's arms.
Content with the life I have led.
Happy that the world is a bit better place,
Because of the blood that I've shed.

He Doesn't Ask Much

He doesn't ask much, neither glory, nor fame,
He knows that history won't remember his name.
He trained to be hard, but he's really quite tame,
And he won't make a fortune, playing this game.
He's a soldier.

He tries to be good, but still gets the blame.
He wants to stand out, but appears just the same.
For the girlfriend who's ditched him, he still bears a flame.
He likes to be proud, but sometimes feels shame.
He's a soldier.

Later in years, he'll probably be lame.
If he's lucky he'll be granted an injury claim.
He may have a medal awarded by some Lord or Dame,
And finally they'll bury him, to a bugle's acclaim.
He was a soldier.

I Hate It When ...

I hate it when my teacher says,
The eight times table must be said,
Then when I can't remember it,
It's the twelve times turn instead.
I hate it when my granny spreads
Cold dripping on her bread,
Then kisses me and the dripping
Forms soft clots upon my head.

I hate it when I open
Christmas presents on my bed,
But instead of getting games and toys,
I get knitted socks so red.
I hate it when my sister
Makes me practise being wed,
Then kisses me and softly says,
"I'll always love you Fred."

I hate it when my mother
Says our kitten must be fed,
Then when I get to where it eats,
It's pooed and quickly fled.
I hate it 'cause my brother knows,
All the things I dread,
And then throws darts at all my toys,
Including Little Ted.

I hate it when my mother
Makes me clean out our coal shed,
And then I have to oil the bikes
And paint our wooded sled.
But the thing I hate the mostest,
That filled my heart with lead,
Was the day the Army told us
That our lovely Dad was dead.

The Professional Soldier

As a truly professional soldier,
Trained to fight and to win in a war,
I was taught there were rules that we had to fight to,
And laws we should never ignore.

We must respect the status of prisoners,
That we capture while winning the fight.
We must always take care of the wounded,
Not matter if we think it's not right.

Civilians must never be targets,
Their homes must be left well alone.
We must always offer compassion,
And attempt for the war to atone.

Hatred is not for professionals.
It's a weakness that may cost you your life.
You must always think of the objective,
And try to ignore all the strife.

No one is saying this is easy.
For as humans we soldiers have fears.
But you have to take care of those by your side,
That you've lived with for so many years.

For if you break the Laws of Armed Conflict,
It's not you that may bear the cost.
Breaking the rules may win battles,
But result in the war being lost.

So take care that you fight as professionals.
Ensure that you don't break the rules.
For a professional can keep his emotions in check,
And that is the best of his tools.

The Unknown Warrior

In the entrance to Westminster Abbey,
Where the kings of England are crowned,
There lies the grave of a soldier,
Who will always be renowned.

The tomb honours The Unknown Warrior,
Who died in the First World War.
His name, number and rank are missing,
No one knows of his regiment or corps.

He was just an unknown soldier,
But he's buried with kings and with lords.
He only carried a rifle and bayonet,
While they all had jewels on their swords.

His body was exhumed from a war grave,
From a battlefield somewhere in France.
He was chosen from a number of bodies,
By a process depending on chance.

No one knows of the suffering he witnessed.
No one knows of the reason he died.
No one knows of the hurt for his family.
No one knows of the tears that they cried.

His tomb serves as the nation's reminder,
Of the soldiers who have died for our sake.
So remember The Unknown Warrior,
And the sacrifices that soldiers must make.

<u>Our Sergeant is Briefing</u>

Our Sergeant is briefing, the what and the why,
When we go into action, someone's going to die.
The men in our section are some of the best,
We will kill when we need to and then capture the rest.

Our weapons are ready, our kit's close at hand,
After the Op, we'll have wiped out the band.
As soon as it's over, I phone up the wife.
Oh balls, I've forgotten where I put my knife.

The kids will be sleeping at home in UK.
We're three hours ahead, it's already Tuesday.
By the time they awake we'll be back in the base.
I'll probably have showered, got the cam off my face.

I've bought them both T-shirts with nice desert scenes,
That will look good with shorts or their favourite jeans.
I know they want Ipads, but out here in the hills,
There's none in the Naafi, or in Buffalo Bill's.

The briefing is over. We check out the comms.
We scribble out letters to our lovers or mums.
A last buddy check and we're out through the gates,
We off into action and we trust in our mates.

Remember We Love You My Son

We know that you're flying into combat today,
And we know that it won't be much fun.
Just take care of yourself and keep out of harm's way,
And remember we love you, my son.

We're thinking of you every hour you're away,
For you life has hardly begun.
You'll feature in every prayer that we pray,
We're so proud of all that you've done.

You will go into battle, as your grandfather did,
And as I did those years long before.
We've watched you grow up and I strongly forbid,
You to suffer in this bloody war.

If you're fighting in Afghanistan or Bombay,
Or some other place under the sun,
Drink only clean water or caffè latte,
And local delights try to shun.

All of your training should keep you okay.
Look after your mates and your gun.
If you're brave you won't get a penny more pay.
Just make sure you come home, my son.

Old Fred had a Girlfriend or Two

We all knew old Fred was soon dying,
A nurse checked the pulse in his wrist.
He knew that his wife had been crying,
As he struggled and clenched his old fist.

Fred whispered to the nurse sat beside him,
"There are many girls that I have kissed.
Some were buxom and others were slim,
But my wife would be top of the list.

There were girls that I yearned for so madly.
There were some that I could not resist.
They were some that I treated so badly,
And a few that I possibly missed.

There was Toni and Margaret and Sue.
There was Lori, Elizabeth and Lou.
There was Ellie, and Catherine too,
And that girl that I met in Peru.

There was the girl that always wore blue,
And the one with the massive tattoo.
There was Linda and Florence and Pru.
There was one that smelt badly of glue.

Another whose roots were Zulu,
And the girl that practised voodoo.
But the oddest one I ever knew,
Was she they called Henry or Hugh.

So now that I bid you adieu,
The last thing that I beg of you,
Is when someone says, "Old Fred Who?"
Tell them, "Old Fred had a girlfriend or two."

No Soldier Looks Forward To Battle

No soldier looks forward to battle,
Or wants to take part in a war.
He dreads the machine-gun's rattle,
From battles fought long years before.
He's not in it for glamour or glory,
Or even for money or fame.
He hopes someone recalls his story,
But normally just gets the blame.

He wasn't the brightest young scholar,
That ever attended his school.
But now knows the worth of a dollar,
And can pick out a sage or a fool.
His collection of beer mats is growing,
He can order a brandy in Greek.
He likes to do training in Cyprus,
In fact, he will be there next week.

His mates let him get the first round in,
Whenever they go into a bar.
They think that his Greek is outstanding,
And like a lift home in his car.
They challenge his fitness each morning,
As they grudgingly run by his side.
But the one thing they share every dawning,
Is an enormous allowance of pride.

He thinks that his mates are the best friends,
That any young soldier could find.
But in truth they'll be there 'til the fight ends,
And protect both his body and mind.
But the people that most care about him,
And worry each time he's away,
Are his parents who worry he looks slim,
And both kiss his photo each day.

John was the Man

Within the battalion, John was the man,
Who gave sound advice and made good the plan.
Respected for smartness, and fitness and drill,
A natural born leader with military skill.
He wore campaign medals for Bosnia and Iraq,
And he'd been on the first anti-Taliban attack.
He was the sergeant that never lost men,
But was made redundant in two-thousand and ten.

Resettlement taught him some good IT skills.
But his job didn't give him the challenge or thrills.
He tried to make friends with the guys in the pub,
But found them so boring, he gave them the snub.
He lived with a woman, who loved his physique,
But soon became frightened of his savagery streak.
He dreadfully missed all his old army mates,
And was often found standing outside the camp gates.

Then after two years he just upped and awayed,
Some thought that he'd joined some foreign brigade.
But the truth was he just couldn't take civvie life,
And he had no support from a family or wife,
So he just opted out and he wandered the towns,
Or lived in the woods like on old Outward Bound.
And eventually an old man with bandaged up feet,
Was found lying lifeless on a cold windy street.

Look Deep in the Eyes of a Soldier

Look deep in the eyes of a soldier,
And take note of all that you see.
You will see lots of pride,
A degree of respect and a love for his family.
You will also see humour and laughter,
And a hint of the joker inside.
And you'll also see the signs of a gentleness,
Especially when the eyes open wide.
And if you stare down deep in the pupil,
You will see a steely resolve,
That shows that once he's committed,
He can tackle all that it will involve.

But if you look that little bit deeper,
Past the eyes that always seem glad,
You will see little hints of the things that he's seen,
That occasionally makes him so sad.
The things that he buries in the back of his mind;
The things that he shouldn't have seen.
The memories he prefers to remember blind,
Of the God-awful places he's been.
So please understand the occasional tears,
And give all the support that you can.
For the soldier will always try to hide away fears,
Because it's what makes him a man.

Mother Woke Up Early

Mother woke up early and was soon out of bed.
She woke up the children and got them both fed.
The girl pulled her best dress down over her head,
And the boy wore his jacket that used to be red,
And they waited for the car in the garden.

Mother held them tight in the cool morning air,
She looked to the corner, but the car wasn't there.
She noticed the edge of her sleeve had a tear,
And tried very hard to smooth the boy's hair,
As his hair gel started to harden.

Mother glanced at her watch, which read quarter to ten,
Then she looked down the road, which was empty again.
The children were aware of her worries and then,
The car turned the corner and the driver stopped when,
He opened the door and asked pardon.

"I'm sorry I'm late, but there's road works back there."
The driver said quietly trying to ignore the hard stare.
"But if we take the High Street, we won't have a care,
And we'll get where we're going, before they're aware,
I was late meeting you in the garden."

They arrived at the church as the clock topped the hour,
As they arrived the rain started to shower.
Then they entered the church, each bearing a flower,
As the flag-draped coffin was marched under the tower,
And the grief in their hearts made them harden.

For the father had died in that faraway war,
That no one knew what he had fought bravely for.
But all in the church felt their hearts badly tore,
By the suffering and pain that his family now bore,
And they fervently prayed for His pardon.

One Man Gently Weeping

The section moved down
The street they were sweeping,
When the Corporal caught sight
Of one man gently weeping.
He crouched as he ran
To the young soldier's side,
Then wrapped his arm over
The man as he cried.
The soldier was knelt
By the remains of a boy,
Who had died holding tight
To his favourite toy.
The Corporal took hold
Of the young soldier's head,
Then stared in his eyes
And he quietly said,

"Don't worry my lad
If you're frightened by war.
If the things that you witness
Are those you deplore.
It's perfectly natural
If you're feeling sad,
It shows that you're human,
Not stark-staring mad.
It's just healthy to hate
Being here on the line.
So catch hold of you breath,
You're just doing fine.
If you are not moved
By the things that you have seen,
Or appalled by the hideous
Places we've been;
If the sight of a body
Is no longer a chiller,
You've changed from a soldier,
My lad, to a killer."

My First True Love

We met long ago and I instantly fell,
For her beauty and charm had me under her spell.
I, a young soldier and she, a young miss,
Both knew it was special from our very first kiss.

We courted, escorted by family and friends,
And soon I declared that my love had no ends.
I saved up the deposit and she chose her ring,
And our families accepted this was no overnight fling.

We hugged and we kissed and we got on so well,
I thought future poets our story would tell.
Every moment together just seemed endless bliss,
One look from her eyes made my blood start to fizz.

Our love, ever stronger, through turns and through bends,
We coped with the heartbreaks that a soldier's life sends.
And I believe that today, we would still be a thing,
If only the Naafi hadn't repossessed her ring.

No Joining Fee Today!

"You should join the British Army lad.
No Joining Fee Today.
Just sign-up on the dotted line
And we'll pay you straightaway.
We'll teach you to be a soldier lad,
And train you in a trade,
So when you return to Civvy Street,
Your life will be well-made."

And I thought of my life in the office,
Which was boring me insane,
Working for Mr. Humphreys,
Who holidayed in Spain.
And I thought of all the glory
And dreamed of all the fame,
And I signed-up on the dotted line
To the Sergeant's warm acclaim.

Soon I began my training,
As a newly signed recruit.
They taught me how to press my kit,
March smartly and salute.
Then after three months training,
As the Corps Band proudly played,
On a cold December morning,
Was our Passing Off Parade.

Mum and Dad stood there so proudly,
As I marched on looking fine.
We did Left Wheel, then Advanced to Front
And Halted all in line.
The Officer Inspecting
Checked the Turn Out of each man,
Then climbed up on the rostrum
And his stirring speech began.

"Every one of you looks splendid.
You're an honour to the Corps.
You'll soon begin Trade Training,
Then it won't be long before,
You're posted to your unit,
Which could be in lands afar.
You'll have fun and travel widely
And soon you'll have a car.

But you will never forget this day,
You became a soldier proud.
So congratulations, one and all,
It's time to cheer aloud.
Here's Hurray for the Royal Signals;
Then we give our Queen Hurray,
And a big Hurray for men like you,
Who we honour on this day."

Then we marched off with our chests puffed out
And pulses beating fast.
And we met up with our Mums and Dads
As the Catterick wind blew past.
I have never felt so wonderful;
I have never felt so good,
I will never feel that way again,
And I guess I never should.

The Recruiting Sergeant had been quite right,
When he told me of the pay.
But what he didn't tell me of,
Was the feeling of that day,
When you become a soldier
And learn a soldier's pride,
As you Pass Off one of the very best,
With others at your side.

A Great Gathering of Men

I have often wondered just how it would be,
If some pub in the country or down by the sea,
Could host a great gathering of soldiers and men,
From each country on Earth and each army in them.
I suspect that initially there would be some distrust,
As they eyed one another, as they stood in the dust.
But then in a while their distrust would abate,
As the drinks started flowing, like rats through a gate.
But I guess that eventually a fight would break out,
When the soldiers had drunk enough Guinness stout.
And the fighting would be quite vicious and gory,
For every soldier was raised on some awful story,
Of injuries suffered in long ago fights,
And battles fought on unscalable heights.
But eventually the strength would drain from each man,
And the heat of the fight would cool off like a fan.
And later a hand would be offered to lift,
The soldier beside him, who he had just biffed.
And then a strong victor would give his new mate,
A glass to be shared with an absence of hate.
Then soon every soldier with his newly made friend,
Would hug one another and all conflict would end.
For every brave soldier is merely a man,
Who will fight for his country, religion or clan.
But when all is said and they've fought one another,
They are soldiers together and each other's brother.

To My Beautiful Mum

To my beautiful Mum and my wonderful Dad,
If you get this letter, things must have gone bad.
But please know that I beg you not to be sad,
For you've been the best parents that I could have had.

I know that you planned that I'd have a career,
And I'd do well at Uni and stay off the beer.
Then train as a pilot or a flight engineer,
And buy a posh house with a big chandelier.

But I joined the Army as a young volunteer,
And passed out of training as a Lance Bombardier.
Now I'm off on patrol, but with pride not with fear,
For we've had the best training and we've got the best gear.

So please think of me kindly and the times we were glad,
For I'll always be with you, as your loving young lad.
And please think of my death as the big launching pad,
That will carry me up to Grandma and Granddad.

Waiting for the Mail

The mother sat in her armchair,
Waiting for the mail.
At this time every morning,
She felt vulnerable and frail.
She dreaded reading bad news
From her youngest soldier son,
Who was serving in Afghanistan
On a field artillery gun.
The letter box clicked open
And the mail dropped with a thud,
There was a letter from her son;
She hoped the news was good.
She read the letter carefully,
Dreading every word,
Her son wrote that they were coming home,
Or so he'd overheard.
There was no need to worry;
He'd got a cushy job,
An observer in Camp Bastion,
Alongside cousin Bob.
The letter gave her happiness
And he signed off with a kiss,
She folded up the letter,
Glad there was naught amiss,
And she cried, and she cried, and she cried.

The son took out her letter
As he huddled in the trench.
A mortar landed close to him
And blew apart a bench.
He ducked a little further down
And glanced at cousin Bob,
Who was just as scared as he was
And had now begun to sob.
This was the fifth barrage they'd had
Since waking up today,
He wished the RAF would hurry up
And blow the foe away.
They all were counting off the days
Until their tour would end.
If this shelling didn't end quite soon,
It would drive Bob round the bend.
A thunderous roar from overhead,
A thump came through the ground,
The jets had hit the enemy
And he so enjoyed the sound.
He lay in the trench 'til ordered out,
Then ran back to his tent,
Then read his mother's letter,
Now crumpled, ripped and bent,
And he cried, and he cried, and he cried.

A Proud Soldier of the Queen

For a decade I have been,
A proud soldier of the Queen,
I have been on tours of duty in Afghan.
I have civvie friends and mates
And I've girls I take on dates,
But my soldier friends I think of as my clan.

There's old Gary and old Bill,
Then there's Barry and there's Phil,
And there's Jimmy, who joined our unit in the spring.
Still, he's keen and he is smart,
Plays good rugby, throws a dart,
And when trouble comes he surely packs a swing.

So have pity on the man,
Who thinks it likely that he can,
Take us on and get away without no pain.
For in combat or at home,
As a unit or alone,
He won't ever want to take us on again.

But don't think that I'm a brute,
'Cause I don't ever want to shoot,
Except when someone is a danger to my mate.
Then I'll do everything I can,
To protect and shield that man,
And make sure the threat lies toes up to his fate.

You can call me any name;
You can hit me 'til I'm lame;
You can shout and scream your insults or your hate.
You can threaten me with pain;
Try to frighten me again;
But don't ever think I will let you hurt a mate.

A Soldier Died Yesterday

A soldier died yesterday,
And no one remembered his name.
No one attended his funeral,
And nobody told of his fame.

For he wasn't remembered by those in the town.
He wasn't remembered by his country or crown.
To some he was just the old man with a groan,
Who they tried to ignore when he started to moan.

But sixty years ago, he had fought in the war,
And people remember the soldier they saw,
Who helped them escape under enemy fire,
Or guided them safely through tangled barbed wire.

They only remembered the face that they'd seen,
With eyes that were hard, but a smile so serene.
Who had willingly offered his dirty rough hand,
And pulled them to safety, without threat or demand.

For in France they remembered the good he had done,
He was fondly remembered for the battles he'd won.
To some he was just the young man with a smile,
Who had tried to improve their lives for a while.

A soldier died yesterday,
And people remembered his face.
No one attended his funeral,
But heaven had kept him a place.

The Last Dance

The dance was a way of escaping,
The privations and horrors of war,
So Brenda put all of her worries aside,
As she danced on the polished wood floor.
The music was lively and cheerful,
She thought it a Glenn Miller score,
Some Royal Artillery soldiers,
Came in through the blacked-out door.

The Artillery soldiers stood looking,
They had recently come back from France.
Brenda smiled back at the soldiers,
But a girl couldn't make an advance.
So she carried on dancing with Alice,
But she did give the occasional glance,
When a soldier tapped her on the shoulder,
And asked, "Could I have the last dance?"

He was, Brenda thought, rather pushy,
And decided to send him away,
But said, "You can have the last dance with me."
Which she hadn't intended to say.
The last dance was sharp at ten-thirty,
The dancers began slowly to sway,
The soldier led Brenda to the dance floor,
Bowed politely and asked, "If I may?"

He held Brenda gently but tightly,
As they slowly moved over the floor.
He asked Brenda her name, then said he was Jim,
Just posted to 3rd Armoured Corps.
Then as soon as the last dance had ended,
He shouted, "Please play an encore."
But the band had started to pack things away,
And she noticed he quietly swore.

"Brenda," he said as he held her,
"It looks like the end of the day.
Would you mind if I walked you home tonight?
But don't worry if your answer is nay."
Brenda thought for only a moment,
Then said, "If it's not out of your way.
I live just off the High Street.
By the park where the children play."

So he escorted Brenda home that night,
And bid her 'Goodnight' at the door.
He asked if he could see her again,
As he would do on many nights more.
His battery then moved down to Hampshire,
In the wet summer of forty-four.
So Jim asked Brenda if she would marry him,
Before he was posted off shore.

The wedding was hurried but tender,
It cost all they were willing to pay.
The honeymooned in an ancient inn,
And made the most of their stay.
Then only a few weeks later,
Jim was once again in the fray,
Fighting ashore in Normandy,
Then battling through the Falaise.

Eventually the fighting was over,
And Jim came back home from the war.
Brenda and Jim settled down to home life,
And Brenda got used to his snore.
They lived in the outskirts of Bristol,
Their first baby slept sound in a drawer,
And many years later, Brenda and Jim,
Couldn't love each other more.

(Continued on next page)

It was summer in the year of two thousand,
When Jim found his cancer by chance,
He had noticed a lump in his armpit,
Which the doctors couldn't stop the advance.
As he lay on his bed in the hospice,
Which the family found hard to finance,
He looked up to Brenda and quietly said,
"My darling, could I have the last dance?"

At the Guardroom Above

The soldier reported to the guardroom above,
And said to the angel, "I'm not good at love.
For years I've been trained in how to do hate,
But please let me in through your big Pearly Gate."

The angel thought hard for a decade or two,
Then said to the soldier, "Here's what you must do.
You must prove that you've led a really good life.
As a soldier you've tried to help people in strife."

The soldier replied, "In peace and in war,
I've tried to be good and a little bit more.
I've always been keen to take care of the weak,
And would shoot anyone who makes fun of the meek."

The angel then said, "But shooting's not good.
You shouldn't solve problems by the spilling of blood.
It's better to show lots of love and compassion,
But I know for a soldier, this has dropped out of fashion."

The soldier was quiet for quite a long while,
Then said to the angel, "I do like your style.
Next time that I get a man in my sights,
I'll give him a kiss and then blow out his lights."

The angel breathed out with a really big sigh,
Then said to the soldier, "I just can't let you by.
I think that you may solve this problem quite quick,
If you pop down to hell and have a chat with old Nick."

The soldier said, "Thanks, but I gave that a try,
And old Nick gave me tests and then gazed in my eye.
He said that he couldn't give me a place down in hell,
For the tests showed that I couldn't do bad very well."

The Homecoming

The C-17 turned for landing,
Carrying its precious load.
And the eyes turned up of those standing,
In long ranks at the side of the road.

The standard bearers checked each other,
And made sure their spacing was right.
Then the crowd edged forward together,
As the Boeing ended its flight.

All eyes turned towards Brize Norton,
And the family bit hard on their lips,
As the hearse appeared round the corner,
And the standards started their dips.

The widow maintained her composure,
And smiled down at her brave little man.
Her son smiled back, and said to her,
"Dad's home from Afghanistan."

After the Remembrance Day Parade

Chard, Somerset 2012

He sat in the bar with his medals all swinging,
After Remembrance Parade, with its memories bringing.
He stared into his glass of warm Otter ale,
And thought of his pals and each one had a tale,
That he would just love, the young ones to tell,
Of those years in the war, when he visited Hell.

So he dropped his head and thought of those singing,
The hymns in the church, when the bells stopped their ringing.
And how his legs ached, but that's just growing frail,
So no complaints to the Lord, just thank him and hail,
'Cause he's now ninety-four, but feeling quite well,
After those years in the war, when he visited Hell.

Then the landlady Lynda came from the bar bringing,
His lunch nicely made and in foil tightly clinging.
"A free meal for you and I'll pay for your ale,
To say thank you for serving, when you didn't fail,
To protect our nation, when others had fell,
During those years in the war, when you visited Hell.

Fire and Forget

'Fire and Forget' in weaponry,
Is the technology of today.
A weapon is aimed and fired,
And quickly zooms away.
The target immediately doomed,
Is simply another kill.
The soldier finds his next target,
As part of his normal drill.

The target ducks and dives,
The weapon follows every move,
Until it destroys the target,
With technology hard to improve.
For the soldier firing the weapon,
The target is then forgot.
He quickly kills the enemy,
Then moves on to his following shot.

But the soldier of yesterday,
Met his enemy man to man.
He saw the face of his enemy,
And fought him to a plan.
He fought him with a rifle,
And fought him with regret.
For the rifle was a weapon,
That was 'Fire and never forget'.

A Soldier's got the Lot

My parents were not wealthy,
For we didn't have a lot,
But my parents always made the point,
"We've paid for what we've got."
We didn't live on pricey food,
We dined on simple fare,
So when I became a soldier,
I already knew to share.

I had never eaten turkey,
Only cowboys ate beef steak.
I had never eaten foreign foods,
Or Battenberger cake.
Then the whole world lay before me,
And I loved to try the new.
I decided I would taste the lot,
Before my days were through.

For a soldier isn't wealthy,
But he lives life to the fill.
His life consists of travelling,
Not always just to kill.
He has friends who'll last a lifetime,
For respect he'd top the pot,
And if you count life's riches up,
A soldier's got the lot.

I am Leading Them to Fight

I am leading them to fight,
On this damp and chilly night,
And the enemy may know we're on our way.
All around me count as friends,
We've been together to all ends,
I must ensure that we don't lose a man this day.

We are closer to them now
And I make this solemn vow,
That I will not risk a life of one of them with me.
I will try to find a way,
To protect them in the fray,
And ensure that all can see the enemy.

There's some dead ground over there,
That with time and usual care,
Will hide us as we move to closer ground.
There's a stream that we must cross,
That should protect us from a loss,
But in crossing it we must not make a sound.

The water's colder than I thought,
With luck a gasp I caught,
That would have warned them we are close to hand.
And the water's deeper here,
But I can see the way is clear,
That will put in the place that we had planned.

Don't let me die.
Don't let me drown.
Don't let me let the others down.
They are braver and much stronger men than me.
Don't let me weaken.
Don't let me fail.
Don't let them see that I am frail.
Oh Lord, up there in Heaven, hear my plea.

If

If you can take praise and ridicule,
And accept that it's all meant in fun.
If you can work hard in a snow storm,
Then a few days later in sun.
If you can leave loved ones behind you,
And focus on what's to be done.
You should think of an Army profession;
You could be a soldier my son!

If you will stand fast with your comrades,
When the fighting around you's begun.
If you will be happy surrounded,
By men who are second to none.
If you will hold ground when the others,
Have panicked and started to run.
You'll be in the proudest profession,
For you'll be a soldier my son.

British Army Rifle 5.56mm

Normal Safety Precautions (NSPs)

Safety Catch on;
Working Parts to the rear;
Holding Open Device;
Check the weapon is clear.

Working Parts forward;
Ensure all the way;
Safety Catch off;
Squeeze the Trigger away.

If the rifle goes Click,
When the Trigger you squeeze,
Safety Catch goes back on,
And you've done NSPs.

My Son Flies Off into Combat Today

My son flies off into combat today.
Oh Lord and your heavenly host,
Please guard and protect him every day,
For he is the one I love most.

I know he's neither an angel nor saint,
He's the first to admit he's got faults.
But he'll fight when others around him would faint,
In German they'd say he's got 'Stolz'.

He's true to his comrades and stands by his mates,
And will never back down from a fight.
He doesn't bear grudges and he doesn't have hates,
And he doesn't have bad dreams at night.

I love him, but know that a pilgrim he ain't,
He can't dance a polka or waltz.
But if somebody tries to put him in restraint,
Please send down a few lightning bolts.

My son flies off into combat today,
Oh Lord and your heavenly host,
Protect all the soldiers while they are away,
But dear Lord, please protect him the most.

Mrs. Brown

Mrs. Brown is the arbiter of fashion,
And the judge of good manners in town.
Maintaining high standards her passion,
Each transgression is met with a frown.

She thinks she's in Sodom and Gomorrah,
If a bra strap can be seen 'neath a gown.
Lewd wear she views as a horror,
And the harlot she'd willingly drown.

Make-up is a threat to the nation,
That could bring her world crashing down.
It should be worn with due moderation,
Or you'll look like the cheapest of clown.

An aberration to this queen of high morals,
Who believes she'd look good with a crown,
Are people who don't sculpture their laurels,
Who are letting the rest of us down.

So please try to live up to her measure,
For Royalty is her favourite noun.
Then you'll bathe in the warmth of her pleasure,
And earn the respect of Ms. Brown.

Looking Forward to Retirement

Ken was looking forward to retirement,
After working for all of those years.
A lifetime of working for others;
A lifetime of worry and fears.

His workmates rushed by him each morning,
A few of them wished him, 'Good day'.
But most of the people ignored him,
As they hurried by him on their way.

But Ken wasn't one for attention,
That a lot of the others found nice.
As long as his family adored him,
He was happy to just pay that price.

His friends didn't know that years ago,
Ken was the toast of the town.
He had joined the Army at seventeen,
To fight for his Queen and her crown.

He was one of the thousands of soldiers,
Who fought in the cold Falklands War.
He landed in San Carlos Water,
To the Argentine bombers' roar.

He won the Military Medal for courage,
As he fired at the jets from the shore.
But the horrors of combat had taught him,
He didn't want to soldier no more.

So he left the Army and settled down,
And eventually made Susan his wife.
They first had a son, then a daughter,
That brought back the joy to his life.

And now on the day of his retirement,
His boss made a really nice speech.
He spoke of Ken's years with the company,
With no mention of that time on the beach.

Life has been so Good

I have been so lucky,
In the way I've led my life.
I have a loving family,
And the most adorable wife.
My father taught me manners
And how to be a man,
And my mother taught me how to cook,
And how to care and plan.

I joined the Army when old enough
In nineteen sixty-five.
I then learned how to work with men,
In order to survive.
I learned to be a soldier first,
In every little way,
And when I look back to those times,
I wouldn't change a day.

I was posted to Western Germany
In nineteen sixty-six,
I learned to drink and fight and swear,
And into trouble mix.
I spent my days with the best of men
And travelled Europe through.
There was scarcely a bar in Germany
That I had not been to.

And then I met my lovely wife
In nineteen seventy-one.
We married and lived in a married pad
And now I had someone,
Who loved me and who wanted me
To become a successful man,
So that we could have a better life,
According to her plan.

Then a few years later,
Our Victoria came along.
The three of us enjoyed a life,
Full of laughter, joy and song.
Then in nineteen seventy-nine
Cyprus became our home.
We loved Greek food and wine and beer,
And sun and sea and foam.

And occasionally I would have to go,
To places not too nice,
To serve my Queen and country,
In combat once or twice.
Then you find the friends you're with,
Will be there when it is bad.
They taught me how to deal with life,
When happy or when sad.

And now I am at ripe old age
And like a rich red wine,
I have a full rich body
And a taste of things divine.
I am thankful to all my friends in life,
And those that have now gone,
So pass the bottle and light a fag,
Let's have a laugh my son.

I am the Common Soldier

I am the common soldier;
I've fought a thousand fights;
I've stood by many heroes;
Not slept on countless nights.

I've fought with clubs and rifles,
Lances, shields and swords.
I've fought for Kings and tyrants,
Republics and rich lords.

I've suffered wounds of every kind,
Diseases, hurts and boils.
I've sometimes starved, ate rubbish food,
Then feasted on the spoils.

I've fought the whole world over,
In many different wars.
I've rescued many virgins,
And then relaxed with whores.

I've fought in many battles,
In many different climes.
I've fought each day in history,
From the earliest of times.

I've faced a thousand crises,
I've conquered countless fears.
I've often thirsted for a drink,
Then drunk a thousand beers.

I've carried wounded comrades,
Sometimes been tenderly nursed.
I've been greeted as a hero,
And then next day I've been cursed.

I've sometimes stood by Princes;
I've sometimes stood by knaves;
I've sometimes stood by cowards;
I've sometimes stood by braves.

I've fought for Adolf Hitler;
I've fought for Mao Tse Tung;
I've fought for the Emperor Constantine,
And all the saints unsung.

I will never be an angel,
But I fight evil when I can.
I will never be a devil,
For I'm just a common man.

So what makes me so different,
That I stand out from the rest?
Just that I have stood in battle,
And I have passed the test.

The Cost of Courage

The Training Sergeant told us,
"Courage we expect!
We've trained you all as soldier,
Our country to protect.
But a soldier's life is not all drill
And I mean no disrespect,
When I tell you, you're paid to fight,
Not just to stand erect."

He then gave us a steely glare
And stood in front of me,
And said, "You've passed a lot of tests
And I can clearly see,
You'll be a credit to the corps,
Wherever you may be,
But you may need some courage,
Which luckily is free."

"For courage doesn't have a price,
It won't cost you a cent.
It can't be bought for millions;
It can't be hired or rent.
Some men just seem to have it;
Perhaps it's heaven sent,
Or perhaps it is inside each man,
Waiting for a chance to vent."

The Sergeant's words I took to heart
And waited for the day,
When I would be in battle
And have the chance to play,
The hero's role, to save a friend,
Or fight to clear the way,
Through a multitude of enemies
And many of them slay.

But in all my years of soldiering,
I never had the chance,
To show I was a hero,
By leading some advance.
So I never had to pay the price,
For taking up a stance,
And showing fearless courage
With my trusty bayonet-lance.

But I have witnessed courage
In the people I have known.
I have seen it in my family's eyes,
When I left them on their own.
I have seen it in a suffering child,
Trying not to groan.
I have seen a thousand heroes
And the courage they have shown.

But through those years I have learned
That courage has a cost.
Rarely there's no suffering
When the battle line is crossed.
For with every bullet fired in war,
Or hand-grenade that's tossed,
There is a price that must be paid
For every life that's lost.

Christmas Gunfire

The British Army has a tradition,
That celebrates Christmas every year.
It is known as Gunfire Breakfast,
And gives the soldiers Christmas cheer.

The first Christmas I spent in the Army,
Was in Yorkshire's Catterick Camp.
I was posted guard over Christmas day,
To patrol in the cold and the damp.

It was nine o'clock in the morning,
When the RSM burst through the door.
He shouted out "Happy Christmas All!"
And slammed his black boots on the floor.

He held a tea urn in his bulging arms,
And poured out large mugs of tea.
Then said, "Here's a cup of Gunfire,
As your Christmas gift from me."

Gunfire consisted of Army tea,
With lots of rum for added taste.
I lay in my bed with my mug in my hand,
As I drank it warmed my waist.

The RSM gave me a long loving smile,
Which just served to fill me with fear.
It was like the smile that a rattlesnake gives,
If you happen to venture near.

"You enjoy your mug full of Gunfire.
You've earned it, my dear little men.
Then wrap up warm in your uniforms,
And report to the guardroom by ten.

Then he flew out the door like a vampire,
And we drank up our rum-flavoured tea.
As I dressed I smiled at the thought,
Santa frightened the hell out of me.

I've managed to stop the Bleeding

"I've managed to stop the bleeding.
The tourniquet is holding tight.
We've called for a medic by radio.
Trust me, it'll work out alright.

I know that your foot looks just awful,
But it isn't as bad as it looks.
I can hear a helicopter coming,
It is one of those Air Force Chinooks.

I think that your boot helped protect you.
But it looks like it needs some repair.
They'll soon get you back to Medical Aid,
And they'll give you a new one back there.

I promise I'll telephone Sandra,
And tell her it's really not bad.
You know that she's proud she's a soldier's wife,
But I think that I'll first ring her dad.

Your face is looking much better,
Now that I've wiped off the cam.
The medics are here with the chopper.
Oh please try to stay with me Sam."

If I look down when I'm Dreaming

If I look down when I'm dreaming,
I'm wearing my old Army boots,
And although they may not be gleaming,
They are better than those of recruits.

Whatever the lady is wearing,
I'll charm her with witty replies.
My uniform may need some repairing,
But my gaze will soon capture her eyes.

In my dreams she will try to seduce me,
With her curves in a tight-fitting dress.
Her figure will stun and reduce me,
To a khaki-clad mouth-drooling mess.

My wife sometimes sees that I'm smiling,
As I lay by her side in our bed.
But she won't see the girl I'm beguiling,
For it's all going on in my head.

Dan

Dan joined the Army aged seventeen years,
And in military skills he stood out from his peers.
Which enabled this soldier to be best recruit,
For his all-round performance and excellent shoot.

He was posted to Munster with 1BR Corps,
And played his own part in the sixties' Cold War.
He first served in Ulster in seventy-three,
But was wounded by gun-fire that damaged his knee.

Promoted to Sergeant in seventy-nine,
He fought in the Falklands, but stood on a mine.
He was always a soldier and incredibly brave,
Who would risk his own life, if a child he could save.

After medical treatment and again fighting fit,
He was posted to Bosnia and landed at Split.
He guarded the weak and protected the frail.
He gave food to the starving and brought them their mail.

He retired from the Army in late ninety-five,
And his military pension was enough to survive.
But his Army career left him damaged and weak,
He carried his scars and was reluctant to speak.

Now alone in his ward he is scared of the nurse,
Who he thinks will mistreat him or do something worse.
He's watching a programme that he thinks very strange,
But he's lost the remote, so the channel can't change.

He hates the cold meals that they serve every night.
He waits for the toilet, but they don't know his plight.
He wonders what Christmas will be like this year,
But has wonderful memories of his Army career.

The Soldier and the Girl

The first bullet cracked over the young soldier's head.
He ran quickly to cover as the other men spread.
The firing was coming from a building ahead,
That stood just across a dried-up river-bed.

His rifle went up and he fired several rounds.
Some hit the building and some hit the grounds.
The air was alive with violent war sounds,
When he noticed the girl, lying scared in the grounds.

The girl held her head and screamed very loud.
She was shaking with fear, her face white as a shroud.
"I must try to protect her." He instantly vowed,
As the earth at her side, with bullets was ploughed.

He waved at the girl and stared in her eyes.
He beckoned to her and she started to rise.
The she started to run, to his shock and surprise,
For he wanted to show, where she was, to the guys.

She was killed as she ran only metres from him.
He knew she was dying, her eyes started to dim.
He raged and he screamed, with a face deadly grim,
Then collapsed in a heap, as his tears burst the rim.

Many years later the soldier now old,
Lay in his bed, close to death, feeling cold.
The girl stood by his side, now not frightened, but bold.
She beckoned, he followed, without being told.

Old John was a Man

Old John was a man I admired all my life.
He was true as a friend and I fancied his wife.
We grew up together and we coped with the strife,
For we learned to be hard and as sharp as a knife.

Old John wasn't big, in fact pretty small,
His chest wasn't thick and he just wasn't tall.
When he was young he would try not to brawl,
For a bully once punched him and left him to sprawl.

But when he grew up John learned how to fight.
He could jab with his left and could punch with his right.
He learned how to deal with a man twice his height,
And vowed not to back down to a man due to fright.

We both joined the Army when eighteen years old.
We struggled through training in the rain and the cold.
We learned how to stick with a hand and not fold,
And life punishes the weak and rewards just the bold.

So that many years later in a land very hot,
We were out on patrol when we heard the first shot.
John faced up to the enemy and stood on the spot,
So we came back from the fight and we left them to rot.

Then just two weeks ago, in our very own town,
A young man challenged John and he wouldn't back down.
I rushed up to the scene and bent down with a frown,
And John simply said, "I think he's taken my crown."

The Old Man's Glass of Whisky

The old man's glass of whisky
Was bigger than yesterday,
But still far short of that required,
To chase the ghosts away.

Last night he'd dreamt of his best friend,
That he so badly missed.
Who had stepped upon a landmine,
And vanished in pink mist.

The empties in his dustbin,
Told their own sad story,
Of just how much he had to drink,
To drown out the cost of glory.

His head was growing heavy,
And his eyes no longer saw,
But his mind was full of painful scenes,
Of the dreadful price of war.

He was found by worried neighbours,
Hugging a cheap whisky blend.
But the smile on his face seemed to say,
He'd rejoined his long lost friend.

The Flag Flying over the House

There's a flag flying over the house today,
As it has for years gone past.
It proudly flutters and flies every day,
At the top of a gleaming white mast.

It shows that the family supports every man,
Who fights for his country and kin.
And will fly for as long as the owners can,
Raise the flag, though their arms grow thin.

It flew on the day that their son went to fight,
For the freedom of Afghanistan.
And it flew at half-mast when they left for the flight,
That brought home the remains of their man.

For their country they buried their son in his grave,
And a volley of shots rang out loud.
The flag flies in honour of the son that they gave,
And their country that makes them so proud.

So never dishonour a flag on a pole,
It can carry a message to all.
It can show that a family remembers the soul,
Of a soldier who answered the call.

Something Brown with Chips

If you ask a British Soldier,
"What do you get to eat?"
He'll say, "We get fresh vegetables,
And a range of tasty meat."
But if you press him further,
He may well walk away,
As what a soldier gets to eat
Will change from day to day.

For in the Army cookhouse,
They try to serve good food.
But ask the chef for details,
And he'll probably be rude.
Ask what soldiers like to eat,
A smile comes to his lips,
He'll say a soldier's favourite meal
Is "Something brown with chips."

For soldiers are not gourmets,
They don't eat from silver plates.
They like plain food, but lots of it,
And share it with their mates.
They don't complain or make a fuss,
Like sailors do on ships,
If the meal that they will eat today
Is 'Something brown with chips'.

There are lots of dieticians
To give advice to Army cooks.
Where the cooks prepare the food
Has many useful books.
The books can tell them how to cook
And may have useful tips,
But all the soldiers want to eat
Is 'Something brown with chips'.

It has been like this for many years
And will be for many more,
For Army food has stayed like this
In peace or times of war.
In World War 2 our enemies
Were the Germans and the Nips,
They just had their Wurst or rice,
Not 'Something brown with chips'.

Then when a soldier comes back home,
His wife gives him a kiss.
She plans to cook a special meal,
That's a gastronomic bliss.
She pours for him a glass of wine,
That he delicately sips,
Then sets before the man she loves,
'Something brown with chips'.

The Heavenly Debate

God and the Devil had agreed to decide,
In one of their weekly debates,
If access for soldiers is always denied,
When they get to the big Pearly Gates.

God said, "Good soldiers abide by the laws,
And fight to defeat evil men."
The Devil said, "Yes, but they fight in my wars,
And do so, again and again."

The Devil said, "Soldiers are all on my side,
They live on, nay thrive on my hates."
But God said, "I make no effort to hide,
That fighting is one of their traits."

The Devil then smiled and admiring his claws,
Said, "So send them all down to my den.
I think that you'll find a good reason or clause,
To condemn them and then say amen."

God adjusted his beard, which was bushy and wide,
And said, "If I check through the dates,
I only fault soldiers for having great pride,
And for fighting to save all their mates."

"But if ever I find that a soldier gives cause,
Or is naughty after I have said "When!"
This soldier will find that he'll end up as yours,
If you'll sign with your bloody red pen."

The Devil went white, then in anger he cried,
"That soldier was one of the greats.
There is nowhere in Hell that a soldier could hide,
My pen that he stole from my gates."

Ruth

Ruth smiled as she walked past her boyfriend,
And made sure her head was held high.
Her boyfriend had been a brave pilot,
Who had fought off the foe in the sky.

Ruth hoped that he saw her go by him,
Although she was now very frail.
But he would not age any further,
He would always be hearty and hale.

He boyfriend had died in his Spitfire,
At the age of a young twenty-four.
He had died defending his country,
At the height of the Second World War.

His grave she had tended for decades,
And replaced all the flowers each week.
She thought of him lying there waiting,
And hoped that one day they would speak.

A few weeks after her ninetieth birthday,
Ruth's health took a turn for the worse.
She went into a hospice with cancer,
For the care of a palliative nurse.

But everyone knew what would happen,
And that Ruth was approaching her end.
Then as her eyes closed for the last time,
Ruth smiled as she walked to her friend.

The Lullaby

(A poem in 2 voices)

"Hush little baby and try not to cry,
I know that you've had a bad fright,
Would you like to hear an old lullaby,
That ought to make everything right."

> "I wish I was home on this awful night.
> Home with my family close by.
> Tomorrow a battle we're planning to fight,
> And some people are going to die."

"Your daddy can't kiss your sweet little head,
For he's a soldier and away at the war.
But I know he would rather be here by your bed,
Or just quietly stood at the door."

> "It will be bedtime now, or shortly before,
> And my daughter, after prayers have been said,
> Will kiss her mother, who I truly adore,
> Then curl up with her favourite Ted."

"Now go to sleep, you'll wake by and by,
Wrap up tight, so the bed-bugs don't bite.
When daddy gets back, he'll want to know why,
You cried for him every night."

> "Sleep tight little one, as you turn out the light.
> Watch the moon and the stars in the sky.
> It won't be long, 'til I'm on the home flight,
> But for now, I will just have to cry."

Lurch

Lurch McCartin was a soldier,
And now his tale I'll tell,
He tried to act so soldierly,
But couldn't do it well.

Lurch drove instructors crazy,
For he wasn't smart or neat.
He lacked communication,
With either of his feet.

His face was always dirty,
He never seemed to shave,
His skin was always spotty,
With the pallor of the grave.

His arms lacked coordination,
With no overall command.
The actions of his right-hand,
Surprised the other hand.

His uniform was crumpled,
His boots had not a shine.
His totally creaseless trousers,
And were not as nice as mine.

If the sergeant ordered "Left Turn!"
Our Lurch turned to the right.
The sergeant then would shout at him,
With all his pent up might.

I thought of Lurch as my best friend,
For as you can clearly see,
Standing on parade by him,
Took all the grief off me.

Our Padre

Our Padre is a geezer man,
A most respected bloke.
He likes to have a beer with us,
And tells a real good joke.
He wears a chaplain's collar,
As well as Captain's pips.
He carries around his bible,
And gives cracking betting tips.

The lads are pleased to see him,
When he drives into our base.
He brightens up the dullest day,
With a big smile on his face.
He leads us in a service;
He prays that we'll get through,
And then he puts his cross away,
And shares a beer or two.

He will listen to our troubles,
And he gives us good advice.
He's the man we can rely on,
When things don't turn out nice.
He knows his soldiers really well,
And he hurts when comrades die,
Then he leads the funeral service,
With silent tears behind each eye.

The Sergeant was Retiring

The sergeant was retiring that morning,
After serving for twenty-two years.
He hoped he had not given warning,
As he wanted to leave with no tears.

He shook hands with men he respected.
He hugged those he cared most about.
He nodded to others, who'd collected,
To watch the old warrior 'Falling out'.

He choked as he shook hands with Harry,
Who had fought by his side in Iraq.
His friend crumpled up his Glengarry,
Then gave him a slap on the back.

"We'll miss you. You ugly old rascal,
But promise we'll all stay in touch."
The sergeant smiled back at McCaskill,
A friend who he'd miss very much.

"Remember the next time you're fighting,"
The old faithful sergeant replied,
"You may find it's a bit more exciting,
Because I am not by your side."

Then they all led him out of the doorway,
As he left to a chorus of cheers.
He would always remember his last day,
And leaving his office in tears.

Tony and Roger

Tony and Roger were deep in debate,
About the prettiest girl in the bar.
Tony said, "Mary drinks beer by the crate,
And then drives me home in her car."

Roger looked round and he pointed at Sue,
And said, "Sue looks lovely today.
She buys me a beer more often than you,
And she dances for Taunton ballet."

Tony took umbrage and started to sulk,
Then said, "But my pension's all gone.
You can drink beer like the Incredible Hulk,
And Sue's neck resembles a swan."

"But look at those legs." Roger replied,
"I think they could do you some harm.
She looks like she's got a fourteen foot stride,
And for me it's all part of her charm."

Tony looked down at his now empty glass,
And said, "It is your turn to buy.
I'll just have a pint of my favourite Bass,
And perhaps I could squeeze in a pie."

Roger shot back, "I'm as hard up as you.
The last round used up all of my cash.
Unless we can borrow, 'til our pensions come through,
I think that's the end of our bash."

But Lynda the landlady leaned over the bar,
And said, "Let me buy you a beer.
I know that you pensions don't go very far,
Even with a full army career."

Together they said, "We've just had a vote.
For the prettiest girl in our town.
And the scrutineers gave us the name on a note,
And fair Lynda, you've just won the crown."

I was Pleased

I was pleased when I left the camp that night,
For a trip to the town with the boys.
The truck took us down to the bar on the right,
That offered us beer, girls and noise.

The truck dropped us off with the bar in sight,
And we dashed off to share in the joys.
The beer tasted good and the lamps shone bright,
As we ogled the girls it employs.

I offered to pay for the first round of beers,
And Steve ordered a pint of the best.
Yesterday Steve picked me up by the ears,
Then playfully stove in my chest.

But today Steve was in a really good mood,
He was laughing and joking with Fred.
I gave him his beer and he said something crude,
And then hit me quite hard on my head.

I shrugged off the pain and returned his smile,
And Steve swallowed a rather large pie.
But after he'd drank and then joked for a while,
Steve gently blackened my eye.

As I dabbed at my eye with a damp piece of rag,
Steve was checking his glass was still full.
I stood up to Steve and I don't like to brag,
But I bruised his fist with my skull.

"Let that be a lesson." I said to Steve,
"I won't take any more of your tricks."
I plucked up my courage and started to leave,
But someone had stolen my sticks.

Mary

May was proud of her husband Jim,
Who had fought in the Falklands War.
She liked being married to a military man,
But he died in two-thousand and four.

Mary was proud of her only son,
They welcomed his birth with champagne.
But although he had great potential,
He died from injecting cocaine.

Mary was left with her cat called Frank,
And the love that she bore him was deep.
But yesterday Frank had a seizure,
And the vet put her loved one to sleep.

Now Mary has no one to care for,
And no one will look after her.
She packs away her cat's little toys,
While listening out for his purr.

Memories

The doctor pulled his chair round the table,
And said, "I'm afraid it's bad news.
But I will give you all the facts I am able,
So just ask any questions you choose."

"You are at the on-set of Alzheimer's disease,
But please put aside all your fears.
Your treatment and drugs hold all of the keys,
And it may not affect you for years."

The doctor went on to tell all that he knew,
Without making it seem any worse.
He ended by booking a monthly review,
Which a doctor would do, or a nurse.

The wife watched her husband's reaction,
And struggled to hold back her tears.
In an effort to force a distraction,
She counted the hairs in his ears.

When the doctor was sure that he covered the facts,
He gave them his visiting card.
The couple walked out with a bend in their backs,
Into rain that was pouring quite hard.

When they got home, he slumped in his chair,
And the wife made him a nice cup of tea.
There were tears in his eyes as he looked up in despair,
And asked, "Why did it happen to me?"

"There are memories that I won't mind losing,
There are others I'll be happy to shove.
But if I maintain a degree of self-choosing,
I don't want to forget all our love."

Our First Date

"John darling, do you remember,
The very first night that we met?
It was ten years ago last December,
On a night so decidedly wet.

We met in a hotel called The Scholar,
Where we both ordered Chilean wine.
I wore my black dress with high collar,
And you said that I just looked divine.

We chatted about love and relations.
You encouraged me up for a dance.
I was just overcome with sensations,
That this was my first true romance.

And now after ten years we're together,
And we live in our lovely new home.
We've come through both good and bad weather,
Just we two and our baby Jerome."

John struggled to remember the occasion,
Then trying so hard not to snub,
With just no attempt at evasion,
Said, "I thought that we met in the pub."

His Parents were soundly Sleeping

His parents were soundly sleeping,
When the knock beat loud on the door.
The mother stared long at her husband.
The clock showed a quarter to four.

The Colonel explained to the couple,
Their son had been shot in the chest.
A surgeon was currently treating him,
The medical team were the best.

Their son was flown home the next morning,
And rushed to the specialist ward.
His parents sped down to the hospital,
While they quietly prayed to the Lord.

By the time they reached his bedside,
Their son had lost his brave fight.
They both stood looking down at him,
The staff sympathized with their plight.

The nurse took them to her office,
And then paying them every regard,
Explained that their son in his wallet,
Had been found with a Donor card.

At first the parents were troubled,
Then accepted the will of their son.
At least some one would benefit,
From the life that was suddenly done.

Later the parents met up with the man,
Heart transplant had brought a new start.
The mother just put her ear to his chest,
To hear once again her son's heart.

Flanders Field

It is one hundred years now,
Since the covenant was sealed,
With the blood of a million warriors,
On the page called Flanders Field.

They didn't want to be there,
But they acted as our shield.
And trusted us to remember them,
Who died on Flanders Field.

They fought for King and Country,
And to death they would not yield.
Their graves are marked by poppies,
That spring up on Flanders Field.

So never forget their sufferings,
And wounds that have not healed.
Then always honour the covenant,
That was struck on Flanders Field.

Harry can't Sleep

Sleep doesn't come easy for Harry,
As he constantly rolls in his bed.
For his dreams are full of memories,
That he just can't shift from his head.

The times when he was frightened,
The times when he suffered pain,
The times when friends were carried away,
Who he would not see again.

He drinks to drown out his memories.
He drinks 'til he falls asleep.
Then he counts the ghosts of those he knew,
Not gently grazing sheep.

Most of his dreams are black and white,
But often they're stained blood red.
Then Harry wakes up in the still of the night,
And talks to his friends who are dead.

He takes pills to sleep when it's lightened,
He knows that he's suffering strain.
The band round his head's ever tightened,
As his head tries to hold in his brain.

He slumps in his chair every morning,
And the chair sags and welcomes him deep.
Then the tears come without any warning,
And Harry sobs as he falls to sleep.

She

She drops off the children at play-school,
Then works in the office for hours.
She rushes to pick up the children,
Then hums to herself as she showers.
She cooks them their favourite supper,
And nibbles the pizza she shares.
She irons their clothes for the morning,
And tells them their Dad still cares.

The children are watching a programme,
About fairies and goblins and bats.
She cleans up the mess in the kitchen,
And then gently talks to her cats.
The children are now getting tired,
For they've had such a very long day.
She puts them to sleep in their bedrooms,
But her thoughts have now drifted away.

She is thinking of her soldier-husband,
Far away in an unmentioned land.
He is fighting to defeat those fanatics,
Whose horrors are carefully planned.
She tries to protect him from worries,
For he has his own worries to beat.
She knows that he'll always love her,
With a love that no one can defeat.

Srebrenica

On an Exercise in Denmark,
A Dutch soldier worked with me.
He was skilled and quite good looking,
As young Dutch men tend to be.

Young Thomas was a sergeant,
Who fought in the Bosnian war.
We had previously met in Kiseljak,
In nineteen-ninety-four.

Our team worked well together,
And young Thomas was a star.
But if Thomas wasn't working,
He'd be drinking in the bar.

I heard that Thomas drank a lot,
And occasionally blew a fit.
For he had been at Srebrenica,
When the Serbs had taken it.

His unit had been captured,
And mistreated by the Serbs.
They were paraded on a vital bridge,
And handcuffed to the kerbs.

They then watched the Serbian soldiers,
Separate the women from the men.
The men and boys were marched away,
And they were never seen again.

Poor Thomas felt he should have fought,
To protect that Bosnian Town.
He drank to drown the guilt he felt,
For letting all those people down.

I later heard young Thomas,
Left the army in ninety-nine.
He then got a job in Eindhoven,
And he was managing just fine.

But then just two years later,
I heard his name once more.
For Thomas committed suicide,
And was found hanging from a door.

Welcome to our Unit

"Welcome to our unit.
I'll introduce you to the men,
And if you're having problems,
You can tell me of them then.
This base is fourteen-Bravo,
But we call it Robin Hood,
The Army won't abandon it,
But the Taliban think we should.

I am Sergeant Higgins,
And he is Corporal Glenn,
You'll be a member of our team,
And your tent is number ten.
The mess-hall is just over there,
And the food is pretty good,
We eat a lot of curries,
But they sometimes taste of mud.

Our boss is Lieutenant Hardy,
And he's wet behind the ears.
We often joke about his youth,
And his lack of service years.
But we all admit he's brainy,
And when the enemy appears,
He is just as tough as any man,
And he often buys us beers.

This is Private Cumberland,
And he has one claim to fame,
For if someone needs a marksman,
His name is in the frame.
But if a prank is sprung on you,
He is normally to blame.
Oh, before we go much further,
Can you tell me your first name?"

"Well, we will call you Rodney,
For we already have a Rod.
He is our vehicle driver,
A valued member of our squad.
Rod doesn't have a lot of words,
He'll just greet you with a nod,
But reads the bible everyday,
And is in close contact with God.

Over there, the naughty twins,
Who are actually not brothers,
But their names appear on orders,
More frequently than others.
If I could have one wish in life,
I'd like to meet their mothers,
So I could tell them face to face,
The advantages of smothers.

So now you've met the Wonder-team,
And I'll let you settle in.
When you're ready for the war,
We'll let the Taliban begin.
Keep your helmet close to hand,
It'll save you from your grave,
And welcome to Afghanistan,
You'll really like it, Dave."

What is a Soldier?

To the enemy he's a target for killing,
Who stands in the way of their rule.
To his classmates he did something thrilling,
But struggled to do well at school.

To his government he accepted the shilling,
And is the cheapest available tool.
To the landlord he pays for his billing,
But often behaves like a fool.

To his girlfriend he is constantly willing,
And in photos he looks really cool.
To his parents he likes food that is filling,
Who they think of as their special jewel.

To his nation he's smart when he's drilling,
But can be a bit of a ghoul.
To his sergeant he is sometimes unwilling,
To carry a load like a mule.

To his comrades he is brave and instilling,
Who'll they'll trust when the going is cruel,
And whenever there's blood that is spilling,
He will drag them alive from the pool.

Some Remembered

His daughters were quietly crying,
As they carried him out of the nave.
His friends were breathlessly sighing,
As they followed him out to his grave.

Some remembered a man in a wheel-chair,
Looking weak and incredibly frail.
Some remembered a youth full of mischief,
Who was lucky to stay out of jail.

Some remembered a good-looking soldier,
Who attracted the girls of the town.
Some remembered a perpetual joker,
Who would willingly act as a clown.

Some remembered a child-doting father,
Who would spend every penny he had.
Some remembered an older grandfather,
Who could sometimes behave rather bad.

Some remembered the wisdom he offered.
Some remembered the jokes that he told.
Some remembered a hand gladly proffered.
Some remembered a youth growing old.

The rain was gently falling,
As they lowered him into his grave.
His comrades were silently calling,
To welcome him back with the brave.

Reincarnation?

If I was offered a reincarnation,
It's a deal that I know I'd decline.
For I don't think my next generation,
Could be any better than mine.

I have lived a life full of laughter,
The bad times outweighed by the good.
It has given me all I was after,
I've enjoyed it far more than I should.

I don't think another would give me,
A life with the friends I have had.
If any of them should outlive me,
I hope they don't think of me bad.

Sometimes I couldn't have been dafter.
Sometimes I have not understood.
I have rarely been called a hard grafter,
But I've done as much as I could.

My family live closely around me,
They have brought joy to my life.
A lot of the ladies astound me,
But the best of the lot was my wife.

I have always been proud of my nation.
I think I've stepped up to the line.
I've had the odd day of frustration,
But the rest of my life has been fine.

Debbie

Eight-year-old Debbie was worried,
Her mummy had been crying again.
She climbed out of bed and she hurried,
To cuddle her mum through the pain.

For daddy was a soldier in Afghan,
Which worried young Debbie a lot.
She checked in the bedroom for Ivan,
Who was snuggled-up tight in his cot.

Mummy helped Debbie climb up on the bed,
And smiled as she stared in her eyes.
The dip in the pillow where mum laid her head,
Was stained from the frequent cries.

Debbie's voice broke as she pleaded,
For mummy to go back to sleep.
But the cuddle was all mummy needed,
And she promised no longer to weep.

Debbie snuggled close to her mother,
And tried to ignore her own plight.
She said that she'd checked on her brother,
Who as always had slept through the night.

She watched her mummy in the dawning light,
And she thought of the daddy she missed.
When he got home she would hug him so tight,
And kiss him, like he'd never been kissed.

What's in a Dream?

I lay on my bed in the barracks,
When he woke with a horrible scream.
My friend sat up straight and said to me,
"I've just had a horrible dream.

I dreamt I'd been whisked up to heaven,
On an incredibly beautiful beam.
And I lay on a bed with a crown on my head,
By the banks of a trickling stream.

An angel smiled down as he told me,
"Heaven works on a wonderful scheme.
Every man has a woman to care for him,
And to feed him with tasty ice cream.

And if you want a change to your diet,
She can cook you a lightly fried bream.
Just shout and beer she will bring you,
As she tries to obtain your esteem.""

In confusion I stared at my buddy,
And said, "So why's that a horrible dream?"
"The woman," he said, "That sat next to my bed,
Was stone-deaf and did not hear me scream."

150

My Poem

My Poem – Mr. John Higgins – 17 years of age

"My mum says that I am just crazy.
Dad says I've got no respect.
My brother says I am too lazy.
Granny says my life is just wrecked.
My teachers said my future was hazy,
Young Sue thinks I'm made out of dough.
My mates think that I'm just a daisy,
But I may give the Army a go."

My Poem – Private John Higgins – 19 years of age

"My sergeant says I'm a disaster,
But he'll make a soldier of me.
My friends say I need to be faster,
If I want a soldier to be.
My knees are now covered in plaster,
I got injured while skiing in France.
I don't think the Army I'll master,
But I think that I'll give it a chance."

My Poem – Sergeant John Higgins – 37 years of age

"The young men they send me are crazy,
They don't have a trace of respect.
The whole bloody lot is just lazy,
And now I've their rooms to inspect.
When given an order, they look dazey,
Not one intelligent man do I see.
If they speak they're always too phrasey.
They are all just so different to me."

Eyes are the Key to the Soul

Words are quite good for conveying,
Hard facts or a carefully thought scheme.
But they're often no good for portraying,
Your feelings or yesterday's dream.

If you ask how a close friend is feeling,
You can guess what they're going to say.
They'll give a look that's revealing,
And then say they are feeling okay.

But we all use a way of surveying,
How somebody feels as a whole.
And it's all really down to the saying,
'The eyes are the key to the soul.'

The eyes tell of suffering and sadness.
The eyes tell of grief with sad tears.
But they also reveal someone's gladness,
And their joys, and their sorrows and fears.

And there isn't a grammar for glances,
That will tell how to read someone's eyes.
We learn by experience and chances,
And in looks we are all really wise.

The eyes of a mother show kindness.
The eyes of a father show pride.
The eyes of a lover show blindness,
To the feelings that they cannot hide.

No one writes poems of what eyes say.
It's not talked of in reference books,
But it's the poetry we see every life's day,
And I think of as the poetry of looks.

A Soldier's Hand

The widow just stares at the picture,
Of her husband looking handsome and grand.
Who marched off to fight for his scripture,
And was killed by a soldier's hand.

For a soldier's hand is hard and rough,
And to some it is truly reviled.
But to some it's the hand of the person they love,
And can't think of it running wild.

To some it's the hand of a friendship,
That they've shared on a hard-fought stand.
Or a comrade they've met on an airstrip,
For a flight to a far-off land.

And to some it's the hand of a reviver,
Reached out by a man who smiled,
As he struggled to reach a survivor,
And grasped hold of the hand of a child.

The Vagrant

The vagrant asked for money,
"To shelter from the rain."
"No!" I said, as I raised my head,
With a look of cold disdain.
Then I noticed the badge he wore,
Pinned proudly to his chest.
He was an Armed Forces veteran,
So one of the very best.

"Did you serve in the Army?"
I asked my new found friend.
"A full career in the infantry,
But they wouldn't let me extend.
The Cheshires was my regiment,
The best there ever was.
I served in many countries,
With a final tour in Aus."

"Then I owe you any favour."
I replied to this noble knight.
"For the Cheshires came and rescued me,
From what I thought my final fight.
I was on a combat tour in Bosnia,
In that country ripped by strife,
When you rescued me from Serbians,
So I think you saved my life."

Will You Go?

England – August 13th 1914

"Herbert dear, I'm proud of you,
But now England's gone to war,
You don't have to join the Army,
Like your father did before.
It's clear I'll always love you,
And in that love you've basked,
But now England needs more soldiers,
Will you go?" His mother asked.

"Mother dear, I love you too,
But I can't ignore this fight.
All my peers have volunteered,
So I must do what's right.
Tomorrow I'll be off first thing,
And each day I'll miss you so,
But my country really needs me,
So you know, I'll have to go."

Ypres – October 18th 1914

"Private Pugh, we've a job to do,
Brigade just has to know,
If there's a path to German lines,
That is clear for us to go.
This mission's very dangerous,
But our company's been tasked,
So I need a soldier I can trust,
Will you go?" The Sergeant asked.

It Won't Be Long Now

Mary looked down at her Harry,
And thought, it won't be long now.
She leaned over her long-suffering husband,
Brushed a lock of his hair from his brow.
At least he was no longer moaning,
He had not made a sound for some time.
She thought of the soldier she'd married,
For Harry looked good in his prime.

Mary glanced at the watch she was wearing,
Harry'd bought it for her in Hong Kong.
The watch face was showing ten-thirty,
But she wondered if it was telling her wrong.
A nurse smiled as she walked past the doorway,
The staff knew what the doctor had said.
But none of them noticed the old soldiers,
That invisibly stood round the bed.

The machine quietly stopped its slow beeping,
And Mary stood up from her seat.
The nurse listened to his chest for a minute,
But couldn't detect a heartbeat.
The nurse looked up and stared at old Mary,
Then cleared Harry's brow with a comb.
She gently sat Mary in the armchair,
And the soldiers welcomed Harry back home.

Dear Mr. & Mrs. Lawrence

Dear Mr. and Mrs. Lawrence,
By now you will know the sad news.
I just can't say how sorry I am,
That Brian was the one we would lose.

I am proud that I served with Brian,
And honoured that he called me a friend.
The only few words I can offer you now,
Is that Brian suffered not at the end.

Brian was a very good soldier,
And had friends you could count by the score.
I know this is not much comfort to you,
But his efforts will help shorten this war.

Brian was the man we would look to,
When the going had become a bit tough.
He had a way of making us laugh,
Although sometimes we saw through his bluff.

We all thought he'd soon be promoted,
He was always at the front of the squad.
I never saw Brian do anything wrong,
So I think he will get on with God.

We have been told that the flight carrying Brian,
Will arrive home on Saturday morn.
And I have the honour to be one of the men,
On whose shoulders Brian will be borne.

The Train

The platform was crowded with people,
Their faces were etched deep with strain.
The doors of the wagon slid open.
They pushed forward to climb on the train.

The young boy had boarded quite early,
He carried his small battered case.
He looked down from the wagon's doorway,
And searched for his mother's kind face.

The boy helped his mother to climb on,
Then looked down in the crowd once again.
He smiled as helped his old father up,
Who was clearly in considerable pain.

The wagon was by now overcrowded,
And the boy struggled to find them some space.
But eventually he stood with his parents,
In at least, the most comfortable place.

The German guard locked the door shut,
Humming an old Schubert refrain.
He signalled all done, then walked away,
From the Poland-bound 'Resettlement Train'.

The Volunteer

The young man was proud of his country,
But had pursued a technical career.
He longed to do something exciting,
So joined the Army as a Reserve Volunteer.

He was trained as an infantry soldier,
And volunteered for a tour in Iraq.
But was soon badly wounded in combat,
With a round in the small of his back.

They flew him back to England,
And he was rushed to a surgical ward.
But the hospital had not treated a soldier,
Who'd been injured while fighting abroad.

He lay in a ward of civilians,
Being treated for minor complaints.
The medics could see he was paralysed,
And kept him secure with restraints.

He felt like an alien stranger,
As he listened to their whines and their moans.
He suffered his own pains in silence,
And thought they were weak with their groans.

He just wanted the company of soldiers,
Who would make his recovery fast.
Not be surrounded by lots of civilians,
Who he personally wanted to blast.

Months later he was home with his parents,
Resigned to a life that he feared.
Unemployed and living on benefits,
How he wished he had not volunteered.

A Soldier's Face

A brow that is furrowed,
By much worry and care,
That proudly stands out,
'Neath a head of short hair.

Two focused bright eyes,
Both alert as can be,
But may have seen things,
That no person should see.

A nose flat by fighting,
That flairs out with each breath,
That knows his love's scent,
And the foul stench of death.

Full lips that can smile,
Or be markedly thin,
As a sign of resolve,
Should the fighting begin.

A mouth wider than most,
With teeth not quite complete,
That can taste victory sweet,
Or bitter defeat.

A chin that juts out,
When he knows he is right,
But can take a good punch,
If it comes to a fight.

Death I Will Fear Thee No More

The old man suddenly sat up erect,
And said, "Death I will fear thee no more.
I've been a true soldier all of my life,
And faced thee oft times before.
I'll admit that you have frightened me,
And caused me sleepless nights,
But the men who I have stood beside,
Kept me safe through all those fights.

So soon I learned how to live with you,
And know that you walked by my side.
You were the evil that lay all around,
From which no one could shelter or hide.
You were the blight that festered away,
That cared not which victims you chose.
Innocent women and children you took,
When you gave them your black bleeding rose.

And now I feel you close by me once more,
And can smell your foul pungent breath.
Your deathly coldness has touched my soul,
But still I will fear thee not Death.
I'm eighty years old and live on my own,
As you've taken my dear darling wife.
Death my old friend, I will fear thee no more,
For now I'm more frightened of life.

The Soldier Cried This Morning

The soldier cried this morning,
As he dressed to go to town.
He didn't know what brought it on,
He just felt really down.
His sobs were pretty quiet,
But the tears were clear to see.
He didn't speak, but turned his head,
And looked away from me.

I didn't know just what to do,
So I turned the other way.
I tried to think of something new,
That I could do or say.
I knew that he had seen some things,
He could not talk about,
That sometimes made him very sad,
And sometimes made him shout.

We stood for many minutes,
In our clothes of green and brown.
I had three stripes on my arm,
And his arm bore a crown.
He fought to hold his tears in check,
And I heard him count to three,
And then he took the deepest breath,
And said something quietly.

I asked him to repeat himself,
In the voice with which I pray.
Then he said, "Let's walk down town."
And I replied, "Okay."
As we walked along he whistled
And I soon began to doubt,
That I had seen this soldier cry,
Who looked so brave and stout.

We walked a little further,
And then he began to frown.
He looked at me, then smiling said,
"I really feel a clown.
You've always been my closest friend,
So now please hear my plea.
If you tell others what you see,
I will crush you like a flea.

In The Straits of Malacca

In the straits of Malacca, I met such a cracker,
I instantly fell for her ways.
Then I sailed to Hong Kong, but we didn't stay long,
And were back in a couple of days.

So I said to Lin Sue, "I truly love you.
I want you to become my wife.
Then I know you won't grieve, if the Navy I leave,
And we settle down to shore life."

So we set life on shore, in old Singapore,
And I got a new job with good pay.
But after some years, and to lots of tears,
I decided we'd move to UK.

So we lived in Skegness and our lives were a mess,
'Cause the chip-shop weren't making no cash.
Then our thoughts would drift back, to the straits of Malac
And with money, we'd been off like a flash.

Now I live on my own, 'cause Lin Su has gone home
And the kids live in Essex and Kent,
And I dream of that day, off the coast of Malay,
When I met my true love, heaven-sent.

What the Hell am I doing?

What the hell am I doing?
Why on earth am I here?
I'm in a front-line position.
My heart is fast-beating in fear.

We know the attack will be coming.
They should be advancing from there.
As soon as the order is given,
I'll light up their front with a flare.

Was that the enemy moving?
I'm aware that I'm holding my breath.
Why aren't I home with the children?
Instead I am frightened to death.

I can see the bastards approaching.
I'll wait just a little while yet,
Then hit them with all we've got going.
This battle they'll never forget.

Take that, you big ugly bastard.
Here's one for the man just behind.
I'll kill everyone with a weapon.
It's all we can do with their kind.

They've broken and now they are running.
But I'll kill 'til they move out of sight.
I can hear my heart beating loudly,
But now from excitement, not fright.

I've checked that nobody is injured,
But they lost at least twenty in vain.
Oh, I love being a soldier in battle,
And pray that they try it again.

The Reunion

The old soldiers met friends of long standing,
With lots of warm handshakes and hugs.
Their friendships were close, not demanding;
Requests met with nodding, not shrugs.

There were drinks being bought by the tray-full,
For friendships that had lasted for years.
The old soldiers grouped tight round a table,
Telling tales full of fighting and beers.

The wives smiled as they listened to stories,
That they wished everyone would forget.
Their husbands remembered old glories,
Or something they'd done for a bet.

They remembered the good times together.
They remembered being soaked in the rain.
They remembered the hot and cold weather,
And forgot all the suffering and pain.

Much later the drinking became slower,
And the chatter began to die down.
The tone of those speaking grew lower,
And foreheads began slowly to frown.

Thoughts turned to those who were missing,
They remembered with fondness and pride.
And their names came with warm reminiscing,
Of old friends who had stood by their side.

That Black-painted Door

Jan came home from the pub that night,
And sat down to watch the late news.
He'd lived in London since after the war,
In a flat in the Battersea mews.

He relaxed in his comfortable armchair,
And within minutes had started to snore.
But after a while, he was startled awake,
When he dreamt of that black-painted door.

He sat up erect and looked round the room,
And noticed a light bulb had blown.
His one-bedroomed flat was tidy and small,
But enough for a man on his own.

He thought of his wife and his children,
Who he thought died in spring forty-four.
But after a while, his thoughts drifted back,
To that dreadful black-painted door.

Was he lucky to survive all the suffering,
That Treblinka had inflicted on most?
Women and children pushed into the room,
Whose faces were his permanent ghost.

He had been chosen to work the gas chamber,
By a man that he could not ignore.
The SS-Scharführer had threatened his death,
With the vicious black whip that he bore.

Jan remembered the screaming had started,
When the pellets were dropped in the vents.
The sound of the wailing of those in the room,
Crescendoed into something intense.

Later the screaming and sobbing died down,
As the victims collapsed on the floor.
Then when the SS gave the order to Jan,
He pulled open the black-painted door.

Tinnitus

The Doc says that I have tinnitus,
Because I have a tone in each ear.
I try to ignore the impairment,
That seems to grow worse every year.

He says that it's caused by the shooting,
That I did in my army career.
We should have been given protection,
Not just cigarette butts in the ear.

It is true that I did lots of shooting,
And we didn't have all the right gear.
We would fire lots of rounds in the morning,
Then go home to a Niagara of beer.

My wife thinks I ignore what she's saying,
But her voice is just not very clear.
My tone seems to match her inflection,
So her orders I don't often hear.

My condition takes some understanding,
For some words I hold very dear.
I can pick up when someone is paying,
For my glass of good ale full of cheer.

It is 4:35 in the Morning

It is four thirty-five in the morning.
I've not slept a wink through the night.
On the table is our Travel Warning,
This evening we'll be catching our flight.

We're deploying to a little known country,
That is threatened by religious extremes.
The zealots lack compassion or pity,
As they seek to impose their regimes.

My wife lies in bed close beside me.
I know that, like me, she's not slept.
She's worried, but hopes I won't see,
The tears that she's silently wept.

The children are sleeping together,
In their bedroom adjacent to ours.
Their room gets damp in cold weather,
Especially in winter's hard showers.

I try hard to forget I'll be leaving.
I roll over and watch my wife's face.
She pretends she's asleep but her breathing,
Is faster than her normal sleep pace.

The alarm clock announces the dawning.
The curtains are surrounded by light.
My wife makes believe she is yawning,
As I get ready to leave for the fight.

He May Be

He may be quietly sitting beside you,
As you sit in the bar with your beer.
Or sleeping outside on the pavement,
As he has now for many a year.

He may be the man with a bearing,
A professional or keen volunteer.
He may be the man that you look to,
When a bully is getting too near.

He may be your father or brother,
Or someone you think of as dear.
He may be your son or your lover,
Or a tramp that you pass with a sneer.

He may be a crook or policeman,
A trained artist or skilled engineer.
He may be a coward or hero,
Or someone whose motives aren't clear.

But he may once have served as a soldier,
Who managed to conquer his fear,
And stood with a handful of others,
When many had fled to the rear.

Janet and her Soldier

When Janet met her soldier,
She had only just left school.
All her friends were jealous,
As they thought it really cool.
To have a soldier boyfriend,
At seventeen years of age,
Made her feel adult at last,
And he earned a decent wage.

They married one year later,
And she became a soldier's wife.
She loved her husband very much,
And liked sharing in his life.
But then he had to go to war,
For the Afghanistan campaign,
She missed him every single day,
Until he was home again.

The she showered him in kisses,
And she hugged him very tight.
She watched him as he fell asleep,
And then watched him through the night.
When the medals were awarded,
She thought she'd burst with pride,
As he had his photo taken,
She stood smiling by his side.

It was barely six months later,
When he woke her up one night.
He suddenly was screaming out,
As his hands gripped her so tight.
Now the nightmares are more frequent,
And he drinks more than he should.
Poor Janet wants her soldier back,
But the outlook isn't good.

Christmas Day in the Cookhouse

It was Christmas Day in the cookhouse,
And the snow was falling fast.
The troops were stood in line outside,
For their Christmas Day repast.

While the chef prepared the turkey,
With its stuffing cooked inside,
He hummed his favourite carols,
And his face was flushed with pride.

The troops burst through the opened door,
Then sat around the Christmas spread.
Some wore new Christmas sweaters,
With Christmas hats upon their head.

The chef served each his dinner,
Then he asked them what they thought,
And each soldier answered, "Very nice."
Then changed the subject back to sport.

The soldiers seemed to like the meal,
And the chef was pleased to see,
They were eating everything in sight,
As they sat around the Christmas tree.

But the chef was happy just to know,
That they'd liked their turkey course,
When a soldier asked that question,
"Have you got tomato sauce?"

The Priest held his Hand

The priest held his hand,
As he struggled for breath,
It was clear to them both,
He was nearing his death.

The priest said, "My friend,
You have nothing to fear.
You've family all round you,
And your children are near.

You have lived a just life,
And you've fought a good fight,
All your years as a soldier,
In a cause that was right.

Now the battle is over,
You can go to your rest.
You have been a good soldier,
And you stood with the best."

Then the old soldier coughed,
And said, "For Christ's holy sake,
That's enough of your sermon,
Let's get on with the wake."

It's a Question

It's a question that's often asked of me,
And one that I've given much thought,
Is evil a thing that is born in a man,
Or something that has to be taught?

Is goodness a thing that we're blessed with?
Is kindness a gift from above?
Is hatred passed on from our parents?
Or just a betrayal of love?

I think that we all have some evil.
I think that we all have some good.
I think that we all fight our battles,
But the outcome is not understood.

For I've seen a bad man love children,
And I've seen a good man show spite.
I have witnessed a man I respected,
Do things that he knew were not right.

So no one can always be perfect,
And no one can always be bad.
We are just a sentient creature,
That has learned from the lessons we've had.

He sits with the other Old People

Dennis has his tea at four-thirty,
And enjoys a nice slice of fruit cake.
He sits with the other old people,
While the nurses are taking their break.
He joins in their small conversations,
And plays games that he played as a child,
But remembers his days as a soldier,
When he was anything other than mild.

He fought in many a battle.
He travelled to countries worldwide.
Now he listens to old people's prattle,
But he still wears his medals with pride.

Dennis sits and he looks out the window,
At a world that he can't understand.
He likes jigsaw puzzles and scrabble,
But finds conversations are bland.
He hates being dependent on others,
But his body is letting him down.
He remembers his days as a soldier,
When he fought for his Queen and her crown.

He's had friendships many would treasure.
He's had adventures beyond others ken.
He has memories that bring endless pleasure.
He's a man that has lived amongst men.

17 Minutes

It has been 17 minutes since she got the call,
But it seems like seventeen years.
It has been 17 minutes since she heard about Paul,
And immediately collapsed into tears.

It has been 17 minutes since she put the phone down,
And tried to collect all her thoughts.
It has been 17 minutes since she felt herself drown,
And the sum of her life came to noughts.

It has been 17 minutes since she was told the news,
That Paul had stepped on a mine.
It has been 17 minutes since she asked for the views,
Of the man on the end of the line.

It has been 17 minutes since she sat on her own,
Not knowing the first thing to do.
It has been 17 minutes since she answered the phone,
And she still can't believe it is true.

"The children will be home at four-thirty,
Should I tell them the truth or just lie?
For some reason I feel really dirty.
Oh, dear God, I just pray he won't die."

The Marks on the Carpet

He looked down at the marks on the carpet,
Where the legs of the table had stood,
And remembered the countless occasions,
When he thought all around him was good.

He remembered the meals with the children,
As he carved up the joint with his knife,
And his eyes were suddenly filled with tears,
As he pictured the face of his wife.

She would always be sat on the same chair,
With her back to the plain kitchen door,
And his mind travelled back to the happier times,
As he stared at the marks on the floor.

She smiled as he always remembered,
In the image that was burned on his brain.
Oh how he missed the woman he loved,
And he whispered, "I love you." again.

He was suddenly aware of the coldness,
And his mind slipped away from his spouse,
As the nurse gripped his arm and led him away,
Saying, "You'll be glad to be out of this house."

You can't call Soldiers Quiet

You can't call soldiers quiet,
Or too modest in their ways.
They like to tell their stories,
And accept the public's praise.
They will tell you of adventures,
In some fabled far-off land,
Or regale you with experiences,
Like burning desert sand.

They will tell you of their romances,
The gorgeous girls they've known.
They will tell you of their daring-does,
The bridges they have blown.
They will tell of foreign countries,
And of bargains they have bought,
But the one thing they won't speak about,
Is the battles they have fought.

For a soldier won't discuss the wars,
Or the horrors that he's seen.
Though he proudly wears the T-shirts,
Of the places he has been.
So don't insult his T-shirts,
That he likes to wear at night,
For it only takes just one wrong word,
And you may have a fight.

Grandfather's Suitcase

There's a suitcase in grandfather's wardrobe,
That looks battered by years of hard use.
It holds all of his treasures and secrets,
Though its straps and its locks are quite loose.

It holds photos and postcards from Cairo.
There are letters with ribbons wrapped round.
There are beer mats from bars all over the world,
With marks from the beers that he's downed.

There's a crumpled old military bible,
That he's carried around all his life.
Inside there's a photo of Grandma,
As a beautiful young-looking wife.

There's a faded old shot of his father,
Dressed up as if going to war.
Then you notice the man in the picture,
Is not seen in the photos no more.

There's a falling-to-pieces old wallet,
That gives off an appalling bad stench,
And inside there's a snap of a woman,
Whose clothes look decidedly French.

His medals are wrapped in a duster,
And are shining and always so clean.
I asked him what makes them so shiny,
And he said, "They were touched by the Queen."

I love sorting through grandfather's suitcase,
As I lie there sprawled out on his bed.
But I know that it just gives a flavour,
Of the memories he has in his head.

His End was Near

The doctor broke the dreadful news,
That his end was near.
The cancer had returned in strength;
He wouldn't last a year.

At first he found it hard to cope,
How do you deal with death?
With his days now fully numbered,
'Til he drew his final breath.

But then one day he thought it through,
For he knew the fate he faced.
If he only had a few months left,
He'd not a day to waste.

He had lots of money in the bank,
And his house was worth a lot,
So he started spending all his cash,
And sold all the things he'd got.

He booked holidays around the world,
And stayed in the best hotels.
He drank and lived a life debauched,
And sometimes slept in cells.

And so he had a wondrous time,
And loved his final year.
Then the doctor broke the dreadful news,
His x-ray now proved clear.

It's Cold

It's cold on the plains of Afghanistan,
As John sits on his Bergen and sips from his can.
He wishes he was home, celebrating New Year,
With his family around him, enjoying a beer.
He hopes they enjoyed all the presents he sent,
As he enjoyed those, which now lie in his tent.
Well next year it's over, he'll be back in UK,
So already John's planning for next Christmas Day.

It's cold on the streets of old Liverpool,
Where Steve sits there shivering, thinking life is so cruel.
All that he's got is now stuffed into bags,
'Cept the cider he's drinking and a packet of fags.
He remembers those days, when he served in Iraq,
With his mates by his side, as they moved to attack.
He can't figure it out, how it all slipped away?
Oh Lord, make it better for next Christmas Day.

I am Proud of my Years as a Soldier

I am proud of my years as a soldier,
And honoured by those by my side.
With the wisdom of now being older,
I can tell you what caused my great pride.

As soldiers we survived harsh conditions.
We lived rough and played rough at times.
We would try to get out of some missions,
Especially those planned for cold climes.

We were clearly not gifted at learning.
We were never the nicest to know.
We spent every pound we were earning,
Our credit was incredibly low.

We were not the best looking of heroes,
But we didn't go out with nice girls.
Our attendance at church averaged zeroes,
And the Army cut off all our curls.

Our drinking was aimed at the gutter.
Our conduct was aimed at the court.
We'd respond to the merest eye-flutter,
We'd drink every drink we were bought.

Now I know this was nothing to boast of,
And I know that I shouldn't be proud.
But we didn't have much to make most of,
And I was only a part of the crowd.

But if ever our country faced danger,
We would fight 'til the last of us died.
And fear was an unwelcome stranger,
This still fills me with a hell of a pride.

He Sat Up Erect

He sat up erect in his hospital bed,
With his slippers lined up by the side.
Hair neatly combed to the side of his head,
His things showed a military pride.

He said to his son in his strong Army voice,
"As a child I was frightened of cats,
And injections and dentists and the obvious choice,
Such as night-things that fly round like bats.

In fact I was frightened of hundreds of things,
Like spiders and cobwebs and worms,
And creatures which had sharp nasty stings,
Or a snake that just wiggles or squirms.

Then I joined the Army and I conquered my fears,
For I'd friends who would keep me from harm.
I forgot how to worry or to burst into tears,
If a plan didn't work like a charm.

We soon had our share of adventurous tours,
But we knew we could trust in our mates.
We proudly wore medals for both Desert Wars,
Though now can't remember the dates.

I gradually got over the things that I feared,
And learned not to be frightened in fights.
A bully was merely a fence to be cleared,
Who backs down when you read him his rights.

So now I believe I have nothing to fear,
No shock that will cause a sharp breath,
The doctor has told me I've less than a year,
But I'm no longer fearful of death."

My Life has been an Adventure

My life has been an adventure,
I look forward to more of the same.
I have had lots of friends as a soldier,
And I hope they remember my name.

I have travelled the whole world over,
And seen more that I dreamt I would see.
I have wonderful memories of those I have met,
And hope they've got good memories of me.

I am proud of the things I have fought for,
And like to think they have survived.
Some people achieve nought in their lifetimes,
Some leave before they have arrived.

So if I have ever upset you,
Or drunk from your glass by mistake.
I would like to beg your forgiveness,
I hope I give more than I take.

Please join me and raise up your glasses,
And together let's all drink a toast,
To the wonderful life of a soldier,
And a friendship that's envied by most.

<u>Do you miss the Army?</u>

A young man came into the pub,
And sat down next to me.
He said, "You were a soldier Clive,
And I can clearly see,
You dearly loved your Army life,
For you tell us constantly,
Stories of all the things you did,
When you served in Germany.

I know that you are now retired,
And living comfortably,
In Somerset, which only lies,
A few miles from the sea.
I know that you like fishing,
And you've got your poetry,
But one thing I would ask of you,
Do you miss the old Army?"

I thought for just a second,
Then I answered earnestly,
"I miss it every breath I take,
And will miss it endlessly.
Right until the day I die,
And then quite possibly,
I'll meet up with my Army friends,
And enjoy their company."

D'you Remember?

D'you remember when we were young soldiers,
And he was our senior recruit,
He helped us to pass our inspections,
And showed us the right way to shoot.
He was also the one to protect us,
If ever we got in a fight,
Especially that time up in Chester,
Which was really a memorable night.

D'you remember that day in the Falklands,
When we went to Whale Point for the day,
And he found some penguins cavorting,
But got frightened and soon ran away?
He pleaded with us to keep silent
But later the secret slipped out,
He had to buy beers for the company,
And we ended up drinking milk stout.

D'you remember when he left the Army,
And we bade him farewell with a do,
We thought he'd do well as a civvy,
When he settled into his life anew?
Then nobody spoke of his family,
His children and beautiful wife,
And nobody mentioned depression,
Or the fact that he'd taken his life.

Spoon (Army Camping) Mark 1

When you join the Army they issue you things,
But the one thing you'll still need my son,
Is that tool that allows you to eat onion rings,
The Spoon (Army Camping) Mark 1.

As a young soldier I watched older men,
Who were experts with bayonet and gun.
They taught me to use the rifle and Bren,
And the Spoon (Army Camping) Mark 1.

You kept it quite handy in pocket or pouch,
And cleaned it when eating was done,
For when food is ready you can't be a slouch,
With your Spoon (Army Camping) Mark 1.

You sharpened one edge for cutting through steak,
Or slicing through stale Army bun,
It was instantly ready for any lunch break,
Your Spoon (Army Camping) Mark 1.

The good ones were square at the handle's end,
For undoing screws just for fun,
And then you'll ready for helping a friend,
With your Spoon (Army Camping) Mark 1.

Some people used them for playing a tune,
But their rattle was something you'd shun.
So keep it to hand for just after noon,
Your Spoon (Army Camping) Mark 1.

I still retain mine after many long years,
And it glistens so bright in the sun.
My favourite tool that I show to my peers,
Is my Spoon (Army Camping) Mark 1.

Carrots

When I was a soldier on the North German Plain,
We'd go out on manoeuvres in sun or in rain.
We would move to location, then move once again,
For all of our moving was how we would train.

But whenever we could we would stay where we were,
And set up our camp, hoping never to stir.
We'd put up our tents, on a hill or a spur,
That was covered in trees, like the spruce or the fir.

And once all was set up, we would give a loud cheer,
Then crack open a bottle of good German Bier.
The taste always smooth, the look always clear,
That wonderful substance that we held so dear.

Then after some days when our rations ran out,
We would call up our Sergeant, with a radio shout,
And make it quite clear, so there wasn't a doubt,
We needed supplies or we were facing a draught.

We had a Codeword that we'd use for our beer.
The Codeword was 'Carrots' and perfectly clear.
We'd ask for some 'Carrots' and to those in our Sphere,
They'd instantly know that we'd run out of beer.

"A dozen nice Carrots." Was a six pack or two.
"A bag full of Carrots." Was lots for our crew.
"Two bags of Carrots." We were planning a do,
And "We've run out of Carrots." We were deep in a stew.

So if you're on manoeuvres on the North German Plain,
And the ground is just soaked by the snow or the rain,
'Carrots' will soon have you feeling no pain,
If your Sergeant is part of the 'Carrot-ing' chain.

Walked the Line

When I took my oath as a soldier,
By signing my name on the line,
I pledged I would fight for my country,
And the town that I think of as mine.
Then when I completed my training,
They sent me across to the Rhine,
And met lots of good looking Mädchen,
Some were gross but many were klein.

We'd train on the ranges at Hohne.
We'd practise with mortars and guns.
We'd stop for our coffee and biscuits,
And sausages stuffed into buns.
We were told we'd be fighting the Russians.
We were only outnumbered by tons.
We'd sometimes watch them on the border,
But they all looked like very weak sons.

And then we were posted to Ulster,
That came as a shock to the spine,
But we were a trained bunch of soldiers,
So everything ought to be fine.
And there we were tested as soldiers,
We were given the chances to shine
I'm proud that I knew so many brave men,
And can say that I once walked the line.

The Grip of a Soldier

If you shake hands with a soldier,
You may be surprised by his grip.
It will be a strong as a sailor,
Who can haul up a decent sized ship.
You may feel the cuts and abrasions,
In the skin of the hand that you shake,
But if the grip is a bond of a friendship,
It's a pledge that the soldier won't break.

The grip of a soldier is binding,
As an oath on the bible is sworn.
The soldier will honour the pledge that he's made,
Lest his word will be treated with scorn.
He'll fight to the death to protect you,
As he knows you will fight so for him,
The battle may be heavy and bloody,
But his word was not gave as a whim.

So treasure the grip of a soldier,
And remember his pledge never ends,
It's the sign of the noble born warrior,
Who eternally fights for his friends.
His friendship will only grow stronger,
As it flourishes year after year,
It can only be won with affection,
And one or two gallons of beer.

The Battle was Deafening and Bloody

The battle was deafening and bloody,
And then he started to scream.
His wife shook his arm to wake him up,
And told him it was only a dream.

He stared without understanding.
Aware of his heart beating fast.
He struggled to think why she'd woken him up,
Then remembered it was all in the past.

His wife cooed some soft words in his ear.
He felt his heart slowing its beat.
He smiled as he looked at his wife so dear,
And loved her for being so sweet.

She brought him a cup of hot chocolate,
Which he drank as it cooled in the cup.
She checked that his mind wasn't troubled,
Then gently she snuggled right up.

Eventually she felt his soft breathing,
And she cried for her husband's great pain.
Then just as her eyes started closing,
The screaming started over again.

Sam - A Royal Engineer

Sam is my mate, and a Royal Engineer,
He can make it, or break it, or shift it to here.
He loved every day of his army career,
And if he had the chance he would re-volunteer.

Sam is proud of his life as a Royal Engineer,
Aiding Coldstreams and Irish and Guards Grenadier.
He also built bridges for a Dutch Brigadier,
Who rewarded their labours with Heineken beer.

Sam went to the Falklands, a mine field to clear,
And lived in Mount Pleasant, for nearly a year.
He visited islands, called Pebble and Shear,
And drove a large crane made for lifting big gear.

Sam has the tattoos of a Royal Engineer,
They start at his ankles and end at his rear.
He has a moustache that droops down in his beer,
And catches the peanuts that he thinks disappear.

One winter it flooded in a town he was near,
So he manned a boat he'd been well-trained to steer.
They gave him the name of the Gay Gondolier,
As he rescued those stranded to many a cheer.

So if you meet old Sam, you must give him your ear,
As he tells you tall stories of his army career,
Of supporting brave troops wearing battlefield gear,
For Sam is still proud he's a Royal Engineer.

Who is that Man?

Who is that man in a T-shirt,
Running for miles around town?
Who is that man with the bright eyes,
And face that is sun-burned and brown?
Who is that man stood there laughing,
Who never appears to be down?
That man is a proud serving soldier,
Who fights for our Queen and her crown.

Who is that man marching proudly,
With men who are equally proud?
Who is that man shouting loudly,
Who always stands out in a crowd?
Who is that man with his head up,
We all know will never be cowed?
That man is a proud serving soldier,
Whose head will refuse to be bowed.

Who is that man in the doorway,
Wrapped up in an old sleeping bag.
Who is that man sitting freezing,
Smoking a thin rolled up fag?
Who is that man with the puppy,
Hoping to sell you a mag?
That man was a proud serving soldier,
Who still stands and honours our flag.

Old Dave

The old soldiers were solemnly filing,
Past those who were stood by Dave's grave,
When one of them found himself smiling,
At a memory he had of old Dave.

He winked at his closest companion,
And asked "D'you remember that day,
When Dave had that fight with O'Banion,
Over something he'd heard Paddy say?"

The other one smiled and then quietly said,
"Yes, but you can't call it a fight.
Dave put his fists up, but was hit on the head,
For O'Banion could slay with his right."

"But when he got back," the first one replied,
"He later informed all the crew,
That he'd spent the night with Paddy's young bride,
Which was what he had planned he would do.

For old Dave simply wasn't a fighter,
And O'Banion really knew how to brawl.
But old Dave was a little bit brighter,
And could easily climb Paddy's wall."

His Memories

He remembers just how it all started,
On that day in Sierra Leone.
They were out on patrol in the jungle,
Once more in a hot danger zone.
They were crossing a small swollen river,
Where the water was warm to the touch,
When firing began from the hillside,
And first did not seem over much.

He remembers that he started firing,
As he looked for some cover nearby.
He remembers he found some protection,
From a rock that was warm and was dry.
He remembers the sound of the bullets,
When they cracked as they flew overhead.
He remembers it suddenly went silent,
And he shouted, "Is anyone dead?"

He remembers a lot of small details,
Of that hot day in Sierra Leone,
When he and his section came under attack,
And the firing was the worst that he'd known.
But the thing he most clearly remembers,
From that day which was noisy and bleak,
Was when one little girl shyly came up to him,
And gave him a kiss on his cheek.

Brothers in Arms

The soldier had been wounded in combat,
And then rushed to the hospital ward.
Two men sat with him as he lay on his bed,
And they both looked as hard as a sword.

A nurse entered the room with her trolley,
And checked that his read-outs were good,
Then looked around at the men in the room,
Who nodded that they understood.

One of them held a book in his hand,
With a finger to mark where he'd read.
The other stood looking down at the man,
Who lay wounded and still on the bed.

The nurse was aware of the hospital rules,
And thought that she'd best ask the men,
Were they related to the wounded young man,
Or just friends of her brave Sergeant Benn.

The man with his finger still stuck in the book,
Told the nurse, from where he was sat,
"We're brothers in arms and you must understand,
We're like family; but closer than that."

Reggie, Kevin, Charlie & Ron

Reggie and Kevin and Charlie and Ron,
Learned to be soldiers and to fight with a gun.
They joined up together and trained as a team,
With their uniforms pressed and their boots all agleam.

They fought in the Falklands and then in Iraq,
They protected each other in every attack.
Then all left the Army in two thousand and one,
That's Reggie and Kevin and Charlie and Ron.

They all lived in London, in Harrow and Hayes,
They worked as a team all of their working days,
Then took turns to pay for the beers in the Swan,
First Reggie, then Kevin, then Charlie, then Ron.

They were still bestest mates after all of those years,
When they shared life together with laughter and tears,
All attended the wedding of Kevin's first son,
That's Reggie and Kevin and Charlie and Ron.

In their later years they still met once a week,
But their drinking was slower than it was at their peak.
Then they all passed away, not at once, one by one,
First Reggie, then Kevin, then Charlie, then Ron.

They are often remembered by their old Army mates,
Who tell lots of jokes amongst heated debates.
Then drink many beers to old friends who have gone,
Like Reggie and Kevin and Charlie and Ron.

197

Harry and Brenda

Harry looked at Brenda
And saw his youthful bride,
A woman tall and slender
Who he longed to lay beside.
Harry felt a sense of pride
For his lady warm and tender,
The lovely vision by his side,
His always soulmate Brenda.

Brenda looked at Harry
And saw her handsome man,
Who she had planned to marry
And things had gone to plan.
She was her husband's greatest fan,
Whose ring she liked to carry.
She could never love another man,
Than her one and true love Harry.

The children see their parents,
As a couple deep in love.
They hope one day to find someone
Who'll fit them like a glove.
Although their parents now are old,
And like to stay at home,
There is no couple more in love,
Or happy on their own.

Joe

Joe and I both joined the Army,
When we were just eighteen years old,
Our parents thought we were both barmy,
But we planned to be famous and bold.
We were posted to bases expected,
And Joe bought a car bright with chrome,
But the car is now standing neglected,
Because Joe won't be coming back home.

We both joined an infantry section,
And trained with the men we thought best.
Then passed through the toughest inspection,
To be posted in wild Baghdad West.
Our base was a run-down old garage,
Our billet was a room filled with trash.
We lived under constant shell barrage,
And Joe saved a fortune in cash.

He planned he would marry his darling,
A girl that lived in the same town,
He would tell us his plans drinking Carling,
As she had just bought her nice gown.
Their wedding would be in the sunshine,
And he planned to pay most with a loan,
But next day he stepped on a landmine,
And so Joe won't be coming back home.

The Guardsman

The Guardsman stood upon parade,
His Bearskin on his head,
His boots were shining brightly,
And his jacket finest red.
He held his rifle on his chest,
Then he gave a little cough,
And nearly had a heart attack,
When his bayonet just dropped off.

The bayonet gave a metallic clunk,
As it landed on the ground,
He felt the eyes of one thousand heads,
As each one looked around.
Each head had turned towards him,
As he tried to hide his guilt,
His Sergeant muttered death threats,
As his soul began to wilt.

The Queen now slowly turned her head,
Until she looked his way.
The parade her yearly highlight,
For it was her special day.
She raised her hand to signify,
She had some words to say,
And an Equerry came running up,
With face of ashen grey.

He listened to his sovereign's words,
Then he saluted to his Queen,
He quickly ran across the square,
To the Guardsman looking green.
He picked the errant bayonet up,
And fixed it in its place,
Then turned about and ran back up,
To the Queen's saluting base.

The Colonel shouted orders,
For the parade to form in line.
Then all turn right and march in step,
As the best troops looking fine.
The Guardsman with his bayonet,
Scarcely had no time to think,
But noticed as he passed the Queen,
She gave a little wink.

Orders have been Issued

The orders have been issued.
The foe is on its way.
The battle lines are recognised,
It will be a bloody day.
The troops are in position,
They are ready for the fight,
Their rifles and machine guns,
Will defend their country's right.

Kevin stands with Michael,
They are hid behind a wall.
Their mission – 'Kill the enemy',
Or at least to shoot them all.
The soldiers form defences,
They will fight 'til they are dead,
Unless their parents call them home,
And send them off to bed.

There are Germans in the bushes,
There are Russians in the street,
There are Zombies all around them,
And the Martians have large feet.
Kevin has his rifle,
And a cutlass in his hand,
If they get near to Lucy,
This will be his final stand.

Home

The aircraft landed early,
They'd cleared customs with no fuss,
The soldiers now sat quietly,
In their White-fleet Army bus.
They'd soon arrive back at their base,
Their tour would then be done.
Some soldiers planned a quiet night,
While others wanted fun.

But one soldier had a worried look,
As he stared at passing towns.
He fretted that he'd meet his son,
Who last time met with frowns.
His son was only four years old,
And after last year's tour,
Had cried when his young father,
Had returned from fighting war.

The soldier with the worried look,
Saw his wife and little son.
As he left the Army coach,
His son began to run.
"I can see my Daddy."
His boy shouted out in glee,
"I've missed you so much Daddy,
Now you're coming home to me."

The Lancers Rugby Team

I'll never play Rugby against the Lancers again,
They really play roughly and mean.
Their Captain rejoices in administering pain,
And their pack is a killing machine.

For the last time we played 'gainst the Lancers,
They chased us all over the field.
They called us a bunch of gay dancers,
Until finally we all had to yield.

One of their players is as tough as old boots,
With looks that would scare any child,
His hair's scary red to its very thick roots,
And his smile is the wrong side of mild.

He plays number seven and we all keep well clear,
His arms look like hammers of steel.
After the match he drinks gallons of beer,
As he troughs down a ginormous meal.

His chest is as hairy as hairy can be,
And his breath stinks of whisky and gin.
His face carries scars that we all can see,
As he gives us his death-laden grin.

I'm frightened to death of this horrible man,
But luckily I can run quicker,
So I dodge number seven whenever I can,
And he's just their Regiment's vicar.

A Soldier's Day

Eight o'clock is breakfast,
Nine o'clock is tea,
Ten o'clock is NAAFI break,
A Sausage roll for me.
Eleven o'clock elevenses,
Twelve o'clock is lunch.
I just like a bowl of soup,
And something brown to munch.
One o'clock it's back to work,
With a nice hot cup of tea,
Two o'clock is fag break,
With my coffee sugar free.
Three o'clock we're nearly there,
A choky bar or two.
Four o'clock last cup of tea,
Before the day is through.
Five o'clock is tea time,
Something brown with chips,
Six o'clock it's time to rest,
Or exercise your hips.
Seven o'clock it's beer time,
Eight o'clock it's Gin,
Nine o'clock it's lots more beer,
Then ten o'clock give in.
Eleven o'clock it's time for bed,
Twelve o'clock asleep,
One o'clock old Jock's loud snore,
Enough to make you weep.
Seven o'clock reveille,
Shower and clear away,
Eight o'clock is breakfast time,
And another busy day.

Her Hero

Jenny had long dreamed of her hero,
Dressed in armour and carrying a sword.
She could picture him on a white charger,
Either a Knight, or a Baron or Lord.
But one evening she bumped into Sydney,
At the pub that stands down the docks,
She discovered that he was a soldier,
Who preferred to wear two different socks.

Sydney wasn't a tall handsome stranger,
But she noticed she laughed at his jokes.
He stood with the other young soldiers,
Who all drank large shots with their Cokes.
His eyes were the first things she noticed,
They sparkled each time that he laughed.
He spoke of adventures and travel,
And told risqué jokes as he quaffed.

In only ten weeks they were married,
And grew used to the other's strange ways.
He liked to have fruit in his porridge,
She liked to go out rainy days.
She was proud of her young-looking soldier,
He was proud of his beautiful wife,
They furnished their new married quarter,
And planned for a long loving life.

It was five years before Jenny noticed,
That he was later and later to bed.
His night-cap grew steadily larger,
He complained of a morning bad head.
She asked if he had any problems,
And he said he was having bad dreams,
Now she holds on to her hero so tightly,
As he shakes and yells out his loud screams.

Johnny

Johnny wants to be a soldier brave,
Just like his old father before,
He looks forward to fighting a battle,
When he marches away to the war.
He will fight for his Mummy and Daddy,
And his sister who is seven years old,
He will always be brave and courageous,
And only do just what he's been told.

John is so proud he's a soldier,
He passed out as best young recruit.
He likes to play sports for his unit,
And excels when they want him to shoot.
He has served on three tours out in Afghan,
He's had friends who were injured or lost.
He accepts all the reasons to fight there,
And never complains of the cost.

Jonnie is still proud of his service,
Though he's now been retired many years,
He has memories of wonderful friendships,
But those thoughts hold both laughter and tears.
He now thinks of the wounds that they carry,
He now thinks of those friends lying cold,
He enjoys meeting mates at reunions,
Whose only regret is they're old.

I Have Been A Soldier

I have been a soldier,
I have lived through wars and crimes.
I have served in many countries,
And in many different climes.

I am proud I was a soldier,
Who stood beside brave men,
And if I could live my life once more,
I'd make that choice again.

I love to meet old comrades,
And hear their tales of old,
Of good times in some foreign bar,
Drinking Carlsberg served so cold.

I have laughed with other soldiers,
And maybe wept sometimes.
I can tell you lots of stories,
By word of mouth or mimes.

But I prefer to tell my tales,
As simple little rhymes.
For the years I was a soldier,
Were the very best of times.

Contents

Title	**Page**
I Have Known	1
Band of Brothers	2
Stand Up and Be Counted	4
Sharing the Life of a Soldier	5
The Colonel was telling a story	6
The Mojave Desert	7
The Saint and the Sinner	8
Every Soldier	9
His Favourite Armchair	10
The Sergeant Recruiter	12
The Soldier Enigma	13
There's a Problem with the Electrics	14
The Guard on the Gates into Heaven	15
There Ain't No Use In	16
When I Die	17
You Can Always Spot A Soldier	18
Wesley	19
When I was a Soldier	20
Sgt. Magonacal Crutch	22
Lest We Forget	24
I Love my 3-inch Mortar	25
The Big Issue	26
I Love Compo Stew	28
The Aircraft will shortly be Landing	29
When You're Young	30
That Certain Feeling	31
The Artist and the Tree	32
I Miss All Those Comrades I Had	35
The Bloody Afghan Desert	36
So what is your Idea of Heaven	37

The Medals on your Chest 38
We were never the Bravest of Heroes 40
Mustaffa 41
Last Man Standing 42
Letter Home – April 1945 43

What Soldiers Do 44
Posted to Afghan 46
Military Intelligence 48
They're Home 49
The Most Expensive Gift 50

When I Die Please Do Not Grieve 52
When You Are Young 53
Yesterday, Today and Tomorrow 54
If You Meet a Soldier 55
Enjoy Your Sweet Dreams 56

I Have Never Told Others Your Secrets 57
I Have Lived Amongst Men 58
Job Interview 59
King Arthur Awakes 60
The Sergeant's Men 62

Let the Children Play 63
Listen 64
Love is not like a Burger 65
A Brave Shoulder of the Queen 66
Autumn's Last Leaf on the Tree 67

Did You Sleep Well My Darling? 68
Christmas in Bethlehem 69
Falkland Islands Grass 70
And the Soldier Cried 72
Don't! 73

Here I Lie 74
He Doesn't Ask Much 75
I Hate It When …. 76
The Professional Soldier 77

The Unknown Warrior   78
Our Sergeant is Briefing   79
Remember We Love You My Son   80
Old Fred had a Girlfriend or Two   81
No Soldier Looks Forward To Battle   82

John was the Man   83
Look Deep in the Eyes of a Soldier   84
Mother Woke Up Early   85
One Man Gently Weeping   86
My First True Love   87

No Joining Fee Today   88
A Great Gathering of Men   90
To My Beautiful Mum   91
Waiting for the Mail   92
A Proud Soldier of the Queen   94

A Soldier Died Yesterday   95
The Last Dance   96
At the Guardroom Above   99
The Homecoming   100
After the Remembrance Day Parade – Chard 2012   101

Fire and Forget   102
A Soldier's got the Lot   103
I am Leading Them to Fight   104
If   105
British Army Rifle 5.56mm – NSPs   106

My Son Flies Off into Combat Today   107
Mrs. Brown   108
Looking Forward to Retirement   109
Life has been so Good   110
I am the Common Soldier   112

The Cost of Courage   114
Christmas Gunfire   116
I've managed to stop the Bleeding   117
If I look down when I'm Dreaming   118

Dan	119
The Soldier and the Girl	120
Old John was a Man	121
The Old Man's Glass of Whisky	122
The Flag flying over the House	123
Something Brown with Chips	124
The Heavenly Debate	126
Ruth	127
The Lullaby	128
Lurch	129
Our Padre	130
The Sergeant was Retiring	131
Tony and Roger	132
I was Pleased	134
Mary	135
Memories	136
Our First Date	137
His Parents were soundly Sleeping	138
Flanders Field	139
Harry can't Sleep	140
She	141
Srebrenica	142
Welcome to our Unit	144
What is a Soldier?	146
Some Remembered	147
Reincarnation?	148
Debbie	149
What's in a Dream	150
My Poem	151
Eyes are the Key to the Soul	152
A Soldier's Hand	153
The Vagrant	154
Will You Go?	155
It Won't Be Long Now	156

Dear Mr. & Mrs. Lawrence   157
The Train   158
The Volunteer   159
A Soldier's Face   160
Death I Will Fear Thee No More   161

The Soldier Cried This Morning   162
In The Straits Of Malacca   164
What the Hell am I doing?   165
The Reunion   166
That Black-painted Door   167

Tinnitus   168
It is 4:35 in the Morning   169
He May Be   170
Janet and her Soldier   171
Christmas Day in the Cookhouse   172

The Priest held his Hand   173
It's a Question   174
He sits with the other Old People   175
17 Minutes   176
The Marks on the Carpet   177

You can't call Soldiers Quiet   178
Grandfather's Suitcase   179
His End was Near   180
It's Cold   181
I am Proud of my Years as a Soldier   182

He Sat Up Erect   183
My Life has been an Adventure   184
Do you miss the Army?   185
D'you Remember   186
Spoon (Army Camping) Mark 1   187

Carrots   188
Walked the Line   189
The Grip of a Soldier   190
The Battle was Deafening and Bloody   191

Sam – A Royal Engineer   192
Who is that Man?   193
Old Dave   194
His Memories   195
Brothers in Arms   196

Reggie, Kevin, Charlie and Ron   197
Harry and Brenda   198
Joe   199
The Guardsman   200
Orders have been Issued   202

Home   203
The Lancers Rugby Team   204
A Soldier's Day   205
Her Hero   206
Johnny   208
I Have Been A Soldier   209

Alphabetical List of Contents

Title   **Page**

17 Minutes   176
A Brave Shoulder of the Queen   66
A Great Gathering of Men   90
A Proud Soldier of the Queen   94
A Soldier Died Yesterday   95

A Soldier's Day   205
A Soldier's Face   160
A Soldier's got the Lot   103
A Soldier's Hand   153
After the Remembrance Day Parade – Chard 2012   101

And the Soldier Cried   72
At the Guardroom Above   99
Autumn's Last Leaf on the Tree   67
Band of Brothers   2
British Army Rifle 5.55mm - NSPs   106

Brothers in Arms   196
Carrots   188
Christmas Day in the Cookhouse   172
Christmas Gunfire   116
Christmas in Bethlehem   69

Dan   119
Dear Mr. & Mrs. Lawrence   157
Death I Will Fear Thee No More   161
Debbie   149
Did You Sleep Well My Darling?   68

Do you miss the Army?   185
Don't   73
D'you Remember   186
Enjoy Your Sweet Dreams   56
Every Soldier   9

Eyes are the Key to the Soul	152
Falkland Islands Grass	70
Fire and Forget	102
Flanders Field	139
Grandfather's Suitcase	179
Harry and Brenda	198
Harry can't Sleep	140
He Doesn't Ask Much	75
He May Be	170
He Sat Up Erect	183
He sits with the other Old People	175
Her Hero	206
Here I Lie	74
His End was Near	180
His Favourite Armchair	10
His Memories	195
His Parents were soundly Sleeping	138
Home	203
How to make a Hero	103
I am Leading Them to Fight	104
I am Proud of my Years as a Soldier	182
I am the Common Soldier	112
I Hate It When	76
I Have Been A Soldier	209
I Have Known	1
I Have Lived Amongst Men	58
I Have Never Told Others Your Secrets	57
I Love Compo Stew	28
I Love my 3-inch Mortar	25
I Miss All Those Comrades I Had	35
I was Pleased	134
If	105
If I look down when I'm Dreaming	118
If You Meet a Soldier	55

In The Straits of Malacca	164
It is 4:35 in the Morning	169
It's a Question	174
It's Cold	181
It Won't Be Long Now	156
I've managed to stop the Bleeding	117
Janet and her Soldier	171
Job Interview	59
Joe	199
John was the Man	83
Johnny	208
King Arthur Awakes	60
Last Man Standing	42
Lest We Forget	24
Let the Children Play	63
Letter Home – April 1945	43
Life has been so Good	110
Listen	64
Look Deep in the Eyes of a Soldier	84
Looking Forward to Retirement	109
Love is not Like a Burger	65
Lurch	129
Mary	135
Memories	136
Military Intelligence	48
Mother Woke Up Early	85
Mrs. Brown	108
Mustaffa	41
My First True Love	87
My Life has been an Adventure	184
My Poem	151
My Poems	2
My Son Flies Off Into Combat Today	107
No Joining Fee Today	88

No Soldier Looks Forward To Battle   82
Old Dave   194
Old Fred had a Girlfriend or Two   81
Old John was the Man   121
One Man Gently Weeping   86

Orders have been Issued   202
Our First Date   137
Our Padre   130
Our Sergeant is Briefing   79
Posted to Afghan   46

Reggie, Kevin, Charlie and Ron   197
Reincarnation?   148
Remember We Love You My Son   80
Ruth   127
Sam – A Royal Engineer   192

Sgt. Magonacal Crutch   22
Sharing the Life of a Soldier   5
She   141
So What is your Idea of Heaven?   37
Some Remembered   147

Something Brown with Chips   124
Spoon (Army Camping) Mark 1   187
Srebenica   142
Stand Up and Be Counted   4
That Black-painted Door   167

That Certain Feeling   31
The Aircraft will shortly be Landing   29
The Artist and the Tree   32
The Battle was Deafening and Bloody   191
The Big Issue   26

The Bloody Afghan Desert   36
The Colonel was telling a story   6
The Cost of Courage   114
The Flag flying over the House   123

The Grip of a Soldier	190
The Guard on the Gates into Heaven	15
The Guardsman	200
The Heavenly Debate	126
The Homecoming	100
The Lancers Rugby Team	204
The Last Dance	96
The Lullaby	128
The Marks on the Carpet	177
The Medals on your Chest	38
The Mojave Desert	7
The Most Expensive Gift	50
The Old Man's Glass of Whisky	122
The Priest held his Hand	173
The Professional Soldier	77
The Reunion	166
The Saint and the Sinner	8
The Sergeant Recruiter	12
The Sergeant was Retiring	131
The Sergeant's Men	62
The Soldier and the Girl	120
The Soldier Cried This Morning	162
The Soldier Enigma	13
The Train	158
The Unknown Warrior	78
The Vagrant	154
The Volunteer	159
There Ain't No Use In	16
There's a Problem with the Electrics	14
They're Home	49
Tinnitus	168
To My Beautiful Mom	91
Tony and Roger	132
Victoria's Met a Hero	22

Waiting for the Mail   92
Walked the Line   189
We were never the Bravest of Heroes   40
Welcome to our Unit   144
Wesley   19

What is a Soldier?   146
What Soldiers Do   44
What the Hell am I doing?   165
What's in a Dream   150
When I Die   17

When I Die Please do not Grieve   52
When I was a Soldier   20
When You Are Young   53
When You're Young   30
Who is that Man?   193

Will You Go?   155
Yesterday, Today and Tomorrow   54
You Can Always Spot A Soldier   18
You can't call Soldiers Quiet   178

Thank you for reading my poems.

Printed in Great
Britain
by Amazon